A year with Yours

Name
Address
Postcode
Home phone
Mobile phone
Email

In case of emergency, contact:

Name
Telephone

USEFUL CONTACTS

BANK	
BUILDING SOCIETY	
CHEMIST/PHARMACY	
CHIROPODIST	
COUNCIL	
CREDIT CARD EMERGENCY	
DENTIST	
DOCTOR	
ELECTRICIAN	
GARAGE	
HAIRDRESSER	
HOSPITAL	
LOCAL POLICE	
MILKMAN	
OPTICIAN	
PLUMBER	
SOLICITOR	
TAXI	
VET	

RENEWAL REMINDERS

	RENEWAL DATE	POLICY NUMBER	TELEPHONE
CAR INSURANCE			
CAR TAX			
MOT			
HOME INSURANCE			
TV LICENCE			
PET INSURANCE			
Yours SUBSCRIPTION			

THE YEAR AHEAD

Why we love...
Spring

RISE AND SHINE

In the UK, there are only three species of mammal that hibernate – the most famous being our beloved hedgehog. As temperatures begin to rise in March, these prickly critters start to wake from their winter-long slumber. The arrival of spring brings a wealth of insects and invertebrates to snuffle up – but leaving out some meat-flavoured cat biscuits and plain water can really help pricklies regain their strength and weight, ready for the breeding season in April.

FRONTLINE FISTICUFFS

Mad March hares are a sign that spring has finally arrived. The brown hare is a typically solitary, nocturnal creature – but thanks to shorter crops at this time of year, you're likely to catch a glimpse of the courtship ritual of hare boxing in fields between March and April. In most instances, it's the female landing the blows, fending off advances from over-amorous males. Some observers have also thought this behaviour to be a test of the male's strength so a female can decide whether they are a good suitor for the mating season. For the best chance of spotting this springtime spectacle, keep a look out for clues such as tufts of fur caught in brambles, or large rabbit-like droppings for a hint that they are nearby.

BLOOMING BLUEBELLS

Spotting a carpet of bluebells is a highlight of any woodland ramble. Early flowering allows them to take full advantage of the sunlight that reaches the woodland floor before other vegetation fights its way to the top. They also produce an important early source of nectar for bees, hoverflies, butterflies and other insects when other flowers have yet to bloom. Bees can sometimes sneakily take all of a plant's nectar by biting a hole in the bottom of the bell. Almost half the world's population grow here in the UK and as well as woodlands, they also grow on hedgerows, shady banks, under bracken on coastal cliffs and on uplands.

NATURE'S CONFETTI

Few sights are quite as uplifting as dormant buds bursting back to life - a promise that the harsh winter months have finally come to an end. Spring is the perfect time to venture into nearby orchards to admire apple, plum and cherry trees in all of their blossoming glory. Head into the countryside and you'll also find a dainty display of tiny white blossoms emerging from blackthorn hedgerows along field edges. Sadly, this period is often short-lived, so it's best to make the most of this dainty display before petals are gone with the wind.

PIC: SHUTTERSTOCK

NESTING NUPTIALS

Right now, British wrens everywhere are busy getting ready for the nesting season. The male wren establishes his breeding territory through a powerful song and will court any female that enters it, tempting her to use one of the many nests that he has built. If, and when, a female chooses a nest, she lines it with moss, leaves, feathers and other insulating materials. A wren's preferred nesting habitat is deciduous and mixed woodland, but you'll also find them in gardens, orchards and farmland hedgerows. They feed largely on tiny insects, but are happy to snack on other high-energy foods such as mealworms and suet balls when natural sources are in short supply.

EGG-CELLENT TRADITIONS

The arrival of spring comes with many unique Easter celebrations. Easter Monday sees northern England taking part in the centuries-old tradition of rolling eggs down grassy banks. Originating in Lancashire, the practice is known as 'pace-egging' and involves decorating hard-boiled eggs which are then rolled down grassy hillsides. Years ago, eggs were traditionally wrapped in onion skins and boiled, giving their shells a golden, mottled effect. But today, they are often brightly painted. The tradition has been running since the 1860s at Avenham Park in Preston, where crowds still gather today. Prizes are awarded for those that roll the furthest or the quickest without cracking.

Spring fling

PICS: NATIONAL TRUST

GAMBOLLING LAMBS

Hardwick Hall grounds, Derbyshire

Nothing lifts the heart like a field of newborn lambs, and Hardwick Hall has plenty of gambolling babies to coo over. The charmingly named 'stumpery' is also home to plenty of spring bulbs, including irises, bluebells and daffodils. Birds to spot include goldcrests, treecreepers, kingfishers and nuthatches. Pack a picnic for a five-and-a-half mile round jaunt with lovely hill vantage points, woodlands and fabulous views of the Elizabethan hall itself.

www.nationaltrust.org.uk/hardwick-hall

BLUEBELL OF THE BALL

Blickling Estate, Norfolk

It's a shame to let spring pass without a wander through one of our prettiest sights – a woodland packed with sweet-scented bluebells. Wondering how to identify native bluebells over their Spanish counterparts? Ours have a strong smell, are a deep violet-blue with white pollen, and almost all of their flowers are on one side of the stem. Blickling has plenty in its charmingly old-fashioned oak, beech and chestnut woods. Try the pleasant four-mile loop from the car park that takes in an 18th Century tower, a Grade II listed ice house and a pyramid-shaped mausoleum.

www.nationaltrust.org.uk/blickling-estate

HOW BLUE WAS MY VALLEY

Rannerdale, Cumbria

While bluebells are usually found lurking secretively in woodlands, visit Rannerdale for a shock of blue splashed across the valleys. It's a lovely area to walk if you're not feeling too fit, as it's one of the smaller fells of the area – and its height didn't stop Alfred Wainwright describing it as 'the best fell top of all'. Walk from the pretty village of Buttermere in a three-mile loop up to Rannerdale Knotts and you can take advantage of views over Buttermere lake and the surrounding hills.
www.nationaltrust.org.uk/buttermere-valley

WATERY WALES

Four Falls Trail, Brecon Beacons

Hunt out the waterfalls of the Brecon Beacons on this famously dramatic walk. You'll see Sgwd Clun-Gwyn 'the fall of the white meadow' as well as Sgwd yr Eira the 'waterfall of snow', which you can even walk behind for other-worldly photos. The area is at its best in spring, with oak and ash woodlands packed with bluebells, anemones and sorrel. Shout into Porth yr Ogof – Wales' largest cave entrance – and listen for echoes. It's a well-marked, circular route from the Gwaun Hepste car park, although it can be slippery so wear sensible shoes.
www.breconbeacons.org/waterfall-country-walking-trails

FENLAND FUN

Wicken Fen, Cambridgeshire

As well as providing an interesting route across boardwalks through pretty fenlands, Wicken Fen is also a top spot for wildlife, especially in spring. Listen out for returning cuckoos and warblers. Keep your eyes peeled for roe deer, as well as the rare Konik ponies (with spring babies!) and Highland cattle which live on the site. Budding botanists should look out for arrowhead and water lilies. See the sights in just under three miles, beginning and ending at the informative visitor centre, and allowing lots of time in wildlife hides en route.
www.nationaltrust.org.uk/wicken-fen-nature-reserve

THIS LITTLE LIGHT OF MINE

The Leas, Sunderland

The Leas is a two-and-a-half mile stretch of cliffs, watched over by the Souter Lighthouse (which can be explored if your legs are feeling up to the 76 stairs!) Spring is the perfect time to visit to witness breeding seabirds including kittiwakes, turnstones, fulmar, cormorants, razorbills, guillemots and purple sandpipers. It also attracts birds of prey and ducks to its wetland habitats, so it's worth remembering your binoculars. The National Trust suggests a two-mile looped route that takes in lighthouse views and a stop off in a birdhide.
www.nationaltrust.org.uk/souter-lighthouse-and-the-leas

All about Alliums

Lucy Bellamy explains the many ways you can enjoy this spring-flowering bloom all year round

Dazzling alliums are often called the firework flower. In every shade of purple, from intense violet to delicate lilac, or even sparkling white, alliums are hard to beat for amazing tones and striking shapes. Allium flowers grow from bulbs and flower in spring. Handily, they can also be bought in pots as shooting and flowering plants that are ready to go, and perfect for popping straight in the soil.

All alliums are brilliant for adding structure to the garden in the border or a pot, with huge, round flowers. Each one is like an explosion, some big, some small, at the top of tall, neat stalks. Plant an allium to flower in spring and it will come back next year and every year after that. They are incredibly reliable, easy-care plants.

There are three main types – the spiky pompom-headed varieties, drumstick alliums with oval-shaped heads which tend to flower later (from July), and edible alliums, better known as chives, with an amazing onion flavour.

Like most early-flowering bulbs, the green leaves are low down on the plant and they do all

the hard work to feed the bulb before the flowers burst open. This makes alliums super-easy to use anywhere in the garden as they can be popped into gaps amongst other plants. They mix readily with lots of different flowers, hovering above their next-door neighbours like purple pom-poms.

In a pot, alliums work well on their own but they are also good companions for other flowers, bringing a bolt of vivid colour and keeping their lollipop shapes much later into the year.

When winter arrives and the plants die back, the spherical dried flower heads will still look attractive in the garden, or can be cut to take indoors to make interesting displays in vases and jugs.

PLANTING IN THE GROUND

The most cost-effective way to grow alliums is by planting bulbs. They need to be planted in autumn to flower the following spring. Individual alliums can look a bit isolated so it's a good idea to plant them in small groups of 12 or more, or even drifts that weave among other plants and link different elements of the garden.

Take note of the eventual size of the flowers – some allium blooms can grow as big as 25cm (10in) across, so you'll need to leave plenty of space between the bulbs. When it does come to planting time, plant the bulbs deeply, at least twice the depth of the bulb. If you plant them too shallow the alliums may topple once they reach their full height.

TO ENJOY THEM NOW

For flowers this spring, buy allium in small pots from the garden centre to plant straight in the garden. Look for plants where the leaves are already pushing up through the compost and there are a few roots peeking out from the base of the pot.

At home, tip the bulbs out of their pots, keeping as much of the original compost around the roots as possible. Sometimes alliums are sold with several bulbs packed in together in one pot. If you find this, plant these as one clump rather than separating them, for an instant display. All alliums need to be planted at the same height in the garden soil or container as they are growing in the pots you buy them in, so be prepared to dig deep if needed.

THREE OF THE BEST FOR GROWING IN POTS

Allium 'Early Emperor'
Beautiful bi-coloured flowers.

Allium Sphaerocephalum
The drumstick allium has pretty purple flowers and a sweet scent.

Allium Atropurpureum
Delicate purple flowers with shining centres.

Modern Gardens, hundreds of easy ideas, projects and fresh inspiration every month.

A colourful

Felt is great insulation, so ideal for this pretty and practical cafetière warmer

YOU WILL NEED

25x21cm (10x8in) of wool-mix felt in beige
Small scraps of pink, yellow, and navy felt
Fading fabric marker
Ruler
Scissors

Glue stick
Small piece of self-adhesive hook-and-loop fastening tape
Sewing machine
Beige polyester sewing thread

coffee cosy

1 From beige felt, cut the main body of the cosy to the depth of the glass area of the cafetière minus 2cm (¾in) and the diameter minus 5cm (2in). For the fastening tab, cut a rectangle measuring 12x6cm (4¾x2½in). However, as cafetières vary in size, you may want to measure yours and cut out your pieces accordingly.

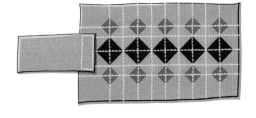

2 Cut five 3cm (1¼in) squares from navy felt, eight 2cm (¾in) squares from yellow felt, and ten 2cm (¾in) squares from pink felt. Arrange the squares on the beige felt as shown, making sure you leave enough space at either end for the tab and the hook-and-loop fastening tape. Use the glue stick to hold the pieces in position.

3 Using the sewing machine and beige thread, sew a grid of straight lines across the design. Each stitched line runs right across the beige felt and across squares from point to point, holding everything in position. Reverse at the start and end of each line of sewing to prevent the stitches unravelling.

4 Pin the fastening tab into position and check that the cosy is a good fit on your cafetière. Then sew the tab in place, stitching in a rectangle around the end.

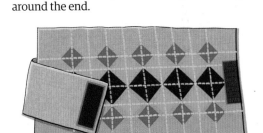

5 Stick the hook-and-loop tape in position, with one side on the front of the cosy and the other side on the back of the tab, and making sure that they align neatly when the cosy is fastened. Then sew the hook-and-loop in place.

Taken from Boho Felt Crafts by Rachel Henderson and Jayne Emerson, published by CICO Books. Photography (c) CICO Books 2018

Why we love...
Summer

SEASIDE SHENANIGANS

As warm weather advances, many of us make a bee-line to the beach to enjoy sun, sea and sand. Many of our coastlines are home to the humble beach hut, which first started out as small wooden structures with wheels used to protect a female bather's modesty. Today, these quirky little huts have been transformed into mini dwellings, some complete with home comforts such as kitchens, beds, armchairs and even toilets! Many beach huts are available to hire for the day. Some of the best locations to spot these British icons are Wells Next the Sea, in Norfolk, Southwold, in Suffolk, Llyn Peninsula in Gwynedd, Whitley Bay in Northumberland and Mersea Island in Essex.
Visit www.beach-huts.com

SUNSHINE, SHOWERS AND RAINBOWS

Whether it's long sunny days, warm showers, or rumbling thunderstorms that you favour - a typical British summer has it all. Alas, it's often the latter - but being in a temperate climatic zone provides the perfect conditions for our plants, insects, animals and ecosystem to thrive to their fullest. With all of that sunshine and precipitation, it's no surprise that it's also the best season for spotting spectacular rainbow displays. This arc-shaped spectrum of light is formed when rays of light hit water droplets, reflecting some of the light back. To see a rainbow, you must have the sun shining behind you and the water droplets in front of you.

PERFECT PAIRING

Strawberries and cream are the epitome of a traditional British summer. The winning combination was served at the first-ever Wimbledon tournament in 1877. This refreshingly sweet treat proved so popular that now an average of 28,000 kilos of English strawberries and around 7,000 litres of cream are consumed at the All England Lawn Tennis Club each year!

Historians believe that the combination of eating strawberries and cream was first started by Thomas Wolsey, an extremely powerful figure in the court of King Henry VIII. It is believed he first served this at a banquet in 1509. Thomas would entertain at least 600 guests at a time, all of whom were fed extravagant feasts twice a day so a dish that didn't need much preparation would have been appealing to the palace staff. Thomas' palace also had a tennis court, where staff served strawberries and cream to spectators. It's thought perhaps this is the reason why we now associate Wimbledon with the dish.

IT'S A BUG'S LIFE

It's easy to overlook the smaller creatures that inhabit our gardens, fields and woodlands. But nothing says summer like the whizzing, buzzing and fluttering of insects in blue skies. One of the most iconic British bugs is the seven-spot ladybird – also known as Coccinella Septempunctata. Their diet largely consists of aphids and other insects, but a few feed on mildews, fungi and plants, too. They hibernate during winter and can be found in cracks and crevices, often in outbuildings and around window frames. Large numbers often migrate here from the continent in warm years, but their numbers have been in decline since the introduction of their harlequin cousins.

BOATING ADVENTURES

There are more than 2,000 miles of navigable inland waterways here in Britain. So, it's no surprise that boating trips and holidays have become a popular pastime. These peaceful highways provide us the opportunity to enjoy a slower pace of life and admire rural views, industrial-era heritage, abundant wildlife and lush green banks. Some of the best scenic canal routes in the UK include the Cheshire ring, the River Wey in Surrey, the Kennet and Avon Canal and – perhaps the most popular - the Oxford Canal.

A COOL DIP

In warm, dry summers, water sources can often be scarce for our wildlife. Help hydrate feathered friends by placing a bird bath in your garden. The RSPB recommends using baths with shallow, sloping sides, a depth of approx 1-4in and a rough surface to prevent birds from slipping in. Be sure to regularly clean your bird bath to remove any debris or droppings and place it somewhere safe with clear visibility, ideally near bushes where they can easily escape if necessary.

Summer fun

PICS: SHUTTERSTOCK

CITY CANAL

Regent's Canal, London

When you think of long walks, a busy city might not be the first location that springs to mind, but actually there are many peaceful pockets of London that are worth exploring. One such spot is Regent's Canal, completed in 1820, which can be followed for around two miles and has a quiet, countryside feel. Watch the canal boats and barges float past; take a peek into the edges of London Zoo and wander past bustling Camden Lock.
canalrivertrust.org.uk

LIFE'S BEACHY

Bolt Head, Salcombe, Devon

For dramatic views and golden sands, Devon is hard to beat. Bolt Head has both in abundance – which explains why it keeps visitors coming back year-round for an easy four-and-a-half mile jaunt. Enjoy looking out over the craggy cliffs before descending to the secluded beach for a cooling paddle. You can then make your way around the jagged rocks and up the Salcombe Estuary, looking out for summer-visiting birds, such as swallows.
www.nationaltrust.org.uk/salcombe-to-hope-cove/

THERE'S NO PLACE LIKE FROME

Frome Valley Walkway, South Gloucestershire

The Frome Valley Walkway covers 18 miles, but don't worry – you can easily break it down into smaller chunks. It passes through a variety of landscapes, from meadows in South Gloucestershire to the wooded valleys south of Winterbourne Down, and into Bristol. The route is home to all sorts of interesting native creatures. While you're unlikely to spot a rare white-clawed crayfish lurking in the water, you might see a kingfisher, dipper or grey wagtail. Alternatively, visit Ridge Wood that's an easy walk from the Walkway, and is packed with wildflowers. Download a free booklet from the link below, or call 0117 922 4325.
www.fromewalkway.org.uk

GEE-UP!

White Horse, North Wessex Downs

British Downs are always at their best during the summer months (and a lot less welcoming when it's chilly!). The North Wessex Downs are a charming spot for a yomp. If you're full of beans, try a six-and-a-half mile walk over easy terrain, that takes in one of Britain's most striking sights – the Uffington White Horse. As well as great photo opportunities of this fine filly, you will also see Uffington Castle, sweeping panoramas and one of the country's oldest thoroughfares.
www.walkingbritain.co.uk/walk-2915-description

ARTHUR'S SEAT, EDINBURGH

Take the high road

Another way to escape the crowds is to head out of busy Edinburgh (particularly bustling during August's Fringe Festival, of course) and up Arthur's Seat. It might not be Scotland's highest peak by any stretch, but it will definitely get your heart pumping as you ascend the roughly three-mile hill walk on one of its various trails. The top is a bit rocky and not ideal for the less able, but if you can manage it you'll be duly rewarded with city views. Edinburgh has various other hills to summit, all in around two hours, including Calton, Castle, Corstorphine, Craiglockhart and Blackford. The more you attempt, the more you can fill up on black pudding or tablet afterwards!
www.visitscotland.com

Pic: National Trust

COLOURFUL TREASURES

Ivinghoe Hills, Buckinghamshire

Britain is home to beautiful butterflies, and there are some rare species to be found in the Ivinghoe Hills. Eagle-eyed walkers might be lucky enough to glimpse Duke of Burgundy butterflies, as well as chalkhill blue, dingy and grizzled skipper, green hairstreak, brown argus, dark-green fritillary, and marbled white (don't you just love their names?) There's a suggested easy two-mile walk that takes in oak woodland, chalk trails and grasslands – perfect for a sunny day.
www.nationaltrust.org.uk/ashridge-estate

IN THE FOOTSTEPS OF GIANTS

Mount's Bay, Cornwall

Children (and big children!) on their summer holidays will love walking across the causeway from Marazion to St Michael's Mount, which takes 10 minutes at low tide. There's a local legend that it was home to a giant who was thwarted by a brave lad, and there's a giant's stone heart to look for, etched in the pathway. Meanwhile, there's an easy two-mile walk along the seawall that's accessible for wheelchairs and pushchairs, and gives fab views across to the Lizard and Mousehole.
www.southwestcoastpath.org.uk

Lovely lupins!

Melissa Mabbitt explains how you can create vivid candles of colour in your summer garden with rainbow-hued lupins

With their gum-drop bright flowers clustering up tall stems like lines of jelly beans, lupins glow with more colours than any other flower. From fizzing lemon-sherbet yellow and bubble-gum pink, to cherry red and deep purple, plant lupins now and they'll be your candy crush all summer.

Choose one with a tangerine or salmon pink hue and it will light up your garden like a flame.

Lemon-yellow lupins look soft and delicate with white partners such as lacy cow parsley and baby's breath, while the dusky colours of blue and amethyst lupins look beautiful in groups, where they'll create a soft hazy look that will make your garden seem bigger.

Grow tall, slender lupins next to floatier flowers that will mingle with their bright spikes, such as hardy geraniums. Let their beautiful star-burst shaped leaves show too. Their soft, fuzzy texture clings on to water after rain, which collects at the centre of the leaves and shines like tiny crystals.

The main flush of flowers is in June or July, depending on the variety, but they will keep flowering until August if you regularly cut off flowers back to a lower set of leaves as soon as they look tired. Don't wait until they have started to form seeds (which look like small pea pods) or they will stop blooming.

These are perennial plants, which means they flower repeatedly, but they may fade away after four or five years. If you let the very last flower spike of the summer turn to seed it will drop to the ground and form baby plants. These will probably change back to the amethyst blue colour of the wild lupin, so if you want to keep your original colour choice you'll need to replace your plants every few years.

HOW TO PLANT

◆ Buy potted lupins in summer from the garden centre and plant them in the ground, in an open spot away from overshadowing trees and shrubs. Choose a sunny spot to get prolific flowers, but they'll still grow well in a partly shady spot.

◆ Lupins are tough plants, as long as they are grown in soil that's on the dry side. They are at their strongest in free-draining soil that's not full of nutrients. They will struggle on heavy, wet soils, but tackle this by putting a few handfuls of grit into the bottom of the hole when you plant.

◆ Dig a hole that's twice as wide as the rootball and the same depth. Add an inch thick layer of grit in the base if your soil is moist rather than well-drained. Place the roots in the hole and fill the gaps around the side with soil. Firm in then wet the soil with at least half a can of water. There's no need to sprinkle plant food around them after planting, as this will lead to lots of leaves and fewer flowers. Also avoid putting too much compost directly on the plant as this can rot the stems.

◆ Newly planted lupins can be susceptible to slug and snail attack, so it's a good idea to scatter some slug pellets around them. If you prefer a more wildlife and pet-friendly option, water on a product such as Nemaslug Natural Slug Killer, available from nematodesdirect.co.uk.

◆ Growing lupins in a container is also a good way to protect them. Once potted you can place the lupin on a graveled area, which will act as a barrier to slugs and snails, or wrap copper tape around the container.

◆ Fill your container with compost and scoop out a hole big enough to take the roots. Place in the hole then firm the compost back around, adding more as needed. Pour half a can of water into the container and water every three days during summer.

Modern Gardens, hundreds of easy ideas, projects and fresh inspiration every month.

THREE OF THE BEST FOR NEON BRIGHT COLOUR

'Manhattan lights'
Fluorescent blooms shine with contrasting plum and gold.

'Salmon star'
Create a coppery orange lick of flame in a border.

'Beefeater'
Deep red flowers flecked with golden yellow make good cut flowers.

Bird and flower

With only the tiniest scrap of sewing required, this pretty summer bunting is so easy to make

YOU WILL NEED

Templates (increased on a photocopier by 200%)
Tracing paper and white card
Pencil
Fading fabric marker
Scissors
3mm ($1/8$in) thick wool-mix felt:
    90 x 100cm (36 x 39in) in red
    90 x 50cm (36 x 20in) each in teal and mustard
Fabric glue
Artist's paintbrush or glue spreader
Pins and sewing needle
Aqua polyester sewing thread
1m (1yd) of cotton twine/yarn

garland

4 Draw around the flower card template onto the mustard felt five times and cut out all shapes. Cut out circles in teal felt, each 3cm (1¼in) in diameter. Cover one side of each teal circle with fabric glue and stick it to the centre of a mustard flower.

1 Trace the templates onto card and cut them out. Place the bird template on the red felt and using the fading fabric marker, draw around it four times. Cut out the shapes. Draw around the wing template onto the teal felt four times and cut out the shapes. Draw around the tail feather template 12 times and cut out the shapes.

3 Draw around the inner wing template onto the mustard felt four times and cut out all the shapes. Cut out 16 small mustard felt circles, each 4mm (³⁄₁₆in) in diameter. Cover one side of each shape with fabric glue and arrange them on the wings and tail as shown. Stick on one mustard circle as an eye for each bird.

5 Arrange all the birds and flowers as you would like them - refer to the photograph as a guide. Lay the cotton twine across the tops of the pieces on the reverse and pin it in place. Overstitch each design to the twine with a few discreet stitches.

2 Cover one side of each wing with fabric glue and stick them to each bird as shown in the illustration. Cover the tail feathers with glue and stick those in place as well.

Taken from Boho Felt Crafts by Rachel Henderson and Jayne Emerson, published by CICO Books. Photography © CICO Books

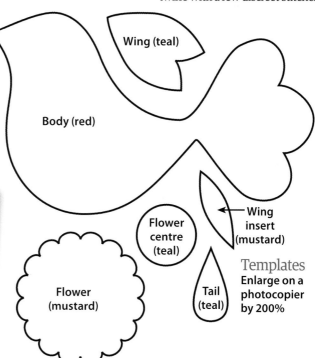

Wing (teal)

Body (red)

Flower centre (teal)

Wing insert (mustard)

Flower (mustard)

Tail (teal)

Templates
Enlarge on a photocopier by 200%

Why we love...
Autumn

ANTLERS AT DAWN

This annual deer rut is one of the most magnificent wildlife sights of autumn. From late September to November the male red deer goes in search of a female mate. This inevitably leads to dramatic fights between two mature males competing to be the dominant stag. Some of the best places in Britain to witness this impressive display are; The New Forest, Hampshire, Exmoor National Park, The Ashridge Estate, Hertfordshire, Margam Park, Glamorgan, Galloway Forest Park, Dumfries and Galloway and Fountains Abbey and Studley Royal, North Yorkshire.

BOBBING FOR APPLES

Did you know that apple bobbing is an ancient autumn tradition that comes from the Roman invasion of Britain? The Romans celebrated Pomona - the goddess of fruit trees and fertility. The native Celts marked their New Year on November 1 with their festival of Samhain. Gradually the two beliefs merged. Apples were closely linked to Pomona, while it was believed that predictions could be made during Samhain. It was thought that anyone who pulled an apple from the water and placed it under their pillow would dream of their future spouse. They also believed that the first person to pick an apple from the barrel would be next to marry!

PRESERVING AUTUMN FRUITS

Make the most of the juicy blackberries clinging to the hedgerows this season by making a super-quick sauce that can be served with ice-cream, yogurt or on pancakes. Put 250g (9oz) blackberries in a pan with 50g (2oz) caster sugar and 100ml (3½fl oz) water in a pan and boil. Simmer till the fruit is soft and add ½ tsp vanilla extract. Tip into a blender and purée then strain through a sieve. Keep in the fridge for three days or in the freezer for up to three months.

WORDS FOR THE SEASON...

"Season of mists and mellow fruitfulness,
Close bosom-friend of the maturing sun;
Conspiring with him how to load and bless
With fruit the vines that round the thatch-eves run."
To Autumn, by John Keats

A CELESTIAL SIGHT

Look to the sky on September 20 for a stunning view of a deep orange full moon! The harvest moon is the name given to the first full moon after the autumn equinox - when the sun shines almost directly over the equator. The term 'harvest moon' originates from when farmers needed bright light to extend their working day. The full moon would light up the sky allowing them to work into the night gathering in the crops in preparation for winter.

CONKERING THE COMPETITION

If you thought a school playground was the only place you'd be likely to see a conker match then you might be surprised to learn that a small village in Northamptonshire is home to the annual World Conker Championships. Held every second Sunday in October since 1965, the championships, in Southwick, near Oundle, Peterborough, draw in around 400 competitors vying to be crowned the world champion and attract more than 5,000 spectators! You'll also find circus entertainers, marching bands, Morris Dancers, craft stalls and much more.
www.worldconkerchampionships.com

BEDDING DOWN FOR WINTER

Right now hazel dormice everywhere are busy getting ready to hibernate through the long winter months. They need to forage for hazelnuts, berries and small insects to help build up their fat reserves to keep them going till spring. The dormouse is an agile climber and mainly nocturnal so is rarely seen. They live in deciduous woodland, hedgerows and dense scrub and spend most of the spring and summer up in the branches rarely coming down to the ground. They hibernate either on the ground - under logs, leaves, in grass tussocks and at the base of trees - or just beneath the ground where the temperature is more constant.

Autumn escapes

TOWER POWER

Stourhead King Alfred's Tower, Wiltshire

What could be better than combining colourful woodland views with a dash of history and even a fine art connection? Tramp through the trees to King Alfred's Tower – a 49m folly built in 1772, it's believed to mark the site where King Alfred the Great rallied his troops in 878. You'll also wander through Park Hill Camp Iron Age Fort and Turner's Paddock – forever immortalised in a 1799 painting by JMW Turner. Not bad for a route that's fewer than six miles!
www.nationaltrust.org.uk/ stourhead/

MISS THE CROWDS

Three Cliffs Bay, Gower Peninsula, Wales

This area is always humming during the summer months, so serious walkers would do well to come after the holidaymakers and plan an autumn jaunt. It's certainly worth the effort as it's constantly winning accolades for its beauty, and was designated the UK's first Area of Outstanding Natural Beauty in 1956. Plus, you won't get bored thanks to its varied terrain of dunes, saltmarsh and limestone cliffs – and look out for the remains of Pennard Castle. Enjoy a four-mile loop from Green Cwm car park.

WET YOUR WHISTLE

Blue Ball Inn, Countisbury, Devon

If the weather is looking iffy make sure you've set off with a hot lunch and a steaming mug of tea inside you! Stopping off at the Blue Ball Inn near Lynmouth means not only can you get a drink, but you can also peruse their suggested walking routes. There are seven walks they recommend, starting from the pub doors, including Winstons Walk – a five-mile route that takes in East Lyn river, National Trust grounds and an enormous badgers' sett. But be warned – it is rather hilly on the second half.
https://blueballinn.com/walking

PIC: SHUTTERSTOCK

A COLOURFUL OUTING

Tobermory, Isle of Mull, Scotland

You might recognise the famously bright, paintbox of houses in Tobermory Bay on the Isle of Mull. One fun way to see them is through a curtain of autumn foliage during a walk that ascends round the edge of the bay for seafront views. There's a three-mile coastal path which also reaches Aros Park and Loch a'Ghurrabain, and has picnic tables along the way in case the weather is kind. Alternatively, head in the other direction to visit Tobermory Lighthouse.
www.visitscotland.com

PIC: NATIONAL TRUST

DOE, A DEER

Ashridge, Hertfordshire

Autumn is an exciting time when it comes to wildlife, and it doesn't get more dramatic than the spectacle of fallow deer bucks knocking antlers to prove themselves to potential mates. Ashridge is also home to muntjac deer, so you might see one of the two species among the trees. No sign of them? Console yourself with stunning seasonal views as the beech, oak and lime trees turn into a blaze of colour. There's a hilly six-mile walk to enjoy that's filled with gorgeous views and picture-perfect scenes.
www.nationaltrust.org.uk/ashridge-estate

FIND SAMMY SQUIRREL!

Glenariff Forest Park, Co Antrim

Keep nice and quiet and your patience might just be rewarded by a glimpse of a red squirrel stocking up for winter in this gorgeous parkland. There are also hen harriers and Irish hare living in the area, so it's worth taking your binoculars. If not, you can still enjoy spectacular waterfalls, autumnal woodland and lakes. There are several trails to choose from, starting from half a mile, but if you've got a bit longer the Waterfall Walkway is worth the effort. It was opened 80 years ago and has had a recent revamp.
https://discovernorthernireland.com

PICS: NATIONAL TRUST, SHUTTERSTOCK, ALAMY STOCK PHOTO

Amazing Asters

Melissa Mabbitt explains how to scatter these gorgeous glowing flowers throughout your autumn garden

While most other flowers are starting to fade, asters burst open to create clouds of shining amethyst colours. These bright, billowing daisy-like plants are the perfect antidote to autumn. Each flower is packed with masses of pink or purple petals around a golden yellow centre, creating a swirl of twinkling stars when they bloom.

There are asters that will sit daintily at the front of a small flower bed, and those that rise up tall behind other plants, adding colour in front of a fence or wall. Some flowers are as small as a five pence piece, others as big as a fifty pence coin.

If you have plants with red or golden autumn leaves, asters add a brilliant splash of purple to create a patchwork of bright colour. They start flowering in September, which is why they are often called Michaelmas daisies, named after the traditional feast day at the end of the month. They'll continue to bloom into November if you choose a late-flowering variety such as 'Purple Dome'. This late flush of nectar-filled flowers will attract butterflies to your garden.

Asters have blooms of every shade of purple, dark violet and burgundy through to bright mauve, blueish lavender, magenta and soft pink. There are red asters and pure white varieties too. They will shine among pink cosmos, Japanese anemones and sedums.

Small varieties grow to just a few centimetres, while tall varieties zoom up to 1.5m, so be careful to check the label for eventual height when you buy them.

Taller plants will look better with small hardy geraniums or a sedum planted in front of them, to hide their lower stems, which can look bare. The smaller varieties are ideal for containers, or for filling the front of a flower bed with glowing amethyst hues.

HOW TO PLANT UP A CONTAINER

You can enjoy asters even if you only have a small patio, deck or balcony, as long as it gets sun for at least half the day.

◆ Choose a large container, such as a vintage zinc bath, and drill several drainage holes into the base before you start.

◆ Add some companion plants such as tall grass to create height or tangerine-coloured Chinese lanterns to set off a purple aster.

◆ Place broken pieces of pot over the drainage holes to stop them getting blocked, then fill the container with a compost such as John Innes No.3. Scoop out enough to make a hole big enough for the roots of each plant.

◆ Place the roots in the hole and firm the compost all around, leaving 5cm of the container rim standing free to allow for watering. Pour half a can of water into the pot, then water weekly until the end of October.

THREE OF THE BEST FOR POTS

'Lady in Blue'
The almost metallic sheen of this aster makes its blue hue really shine.

'Blue Lapis'
Large purple flowers have bright golden centres with masses of petals.

'Sapphire'
This easy aster will form a neat ball covered in purple flowers.

Modern Gardens, hundreds of easy ideas, projects and fresh inspiration every month.

Paper apples and pears

Make these pretty fruit ornaments from old or unwanted books

YOU WILL NEED

Old book without its cover
Pencil
Tracing paper
Cutting mat
Craft knife
Glue and a glue stick

Taken from Book Art by Clare Youngs, published by CICO Books. Photography (c) CICO Books 2018

1 To make the pear, take a section of the old book measuring approx. 1cm (½ in) across the spine.

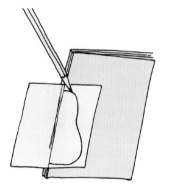

2 Draw the shape of half a pear onto tracing paper using the pencil. Transfer the shape onto the book section, making sure that the straight part of the trace is on the folded spine section of the book. Trace two leaves and a stalk, and then set these aside.

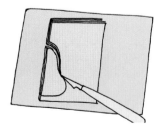

3 Put the book section on the cutting mat and, with the craft knife, cut out the half-pear shape, making sure that you cut through all the pages of the book.

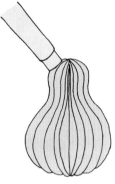

4 Fan out the half-pear shape to make a complete pear form. Put some dabs of glue along the edges of the first page and stick it to the last page to secure the shape in place.

5 Using the traced templates, cut out two leaves and a stalk from another page of the book. Position the stalk between a couple of the pages at the top centre of the pear and secure with a blob of glue. Do the same with the two leaves, one on either side of the stalk. To make the apple, follow exactly the same method but with an apple shape.

Why we love...
Winter

FALLING FOR WATER

Late winter is an excellent time to go waterfall-watching. As snow and ice thaw from the highest peaks, streams swell and waterfalls overflow with thunderous crashing of melting water. The bare tree branches also allow for a better view of the more complex cascades that summer foliage often hides. During especially long, severe winters, the falls can be frozen into silence, with sheets of ice paused mid-flow, creating amazing icicle formations. Some of the UK's most impressive winter waterfalls include Pistyll Rhaeadr in Wales, Kinder Downfall in the Peak District, Ritson's Force in the Lake District and Plodda Falls in Scotland.

SEEING REDS

The Cairngorms National Park in the Scottish Highlands is a stronghold for our native red squirrel, where they inhabit both pine forests and broadleaved woodland. In the winter, they make several nests called 'dreys', built with twigs 6cm (3in) above the ground in holes in trees or set between trunks and branches. They are lined with moss and grass and stripped bark is often collected as bedding material. In winter, a red squirrel's diet consists of spruce and pine seeds, hazelnuts, acorns and berries, fungi, bark and sap tissue, often buried beneath the snow away from the sight of birds. They mate between January and March and have litters of up to four kittens at a time.

MAGICAL MORNINGS

With low temperatures and clear skies come those crisp, sunny, frosty mornings that turn the harsh months of winter into a delight. One of the most magical types of frost to be seen at this time of year is the hoar frost. This feathery frost forms when the water vapour in the air comes into contact with solid surfaces that are already below freezing point. Ice crystals form immediately, and the ice continues to grow as more vapour is frozen. On a still night, it can grow well on tree branches, where the surface temperature is unlikely to rise above zero for many hours. The word "hoar" comes from an old English term for describing the appearance of old age. The white ice crystals that are formed often resemble white hair or beards!

WINTER SOLSTICE

Each year, between December 19-22, thousands of people gather in Wiltshire in the early morning to watch the sun rise over Stonehenge. The Winter Solstice occurs when the North Pole is tilted farthest away from the sun, giving us the shortest day and the longest night of the year and marking the start of astronomical winter. The Stonehenge monument, built in 3,000 to 2,000 BC – shows how carefully our ancestors watched the sun and how heavily they relied upon astronomical observations to time the breeding of their animals, the sowing of crops and the metering of winter reserves between harvests.

NEW YEAR, NEW LUCK

From setting things on fire, to jumping in the river, the Scottish Hogmanay celebration is legendary across the globe. One of the most traditional events includes First Footing – a custom which takes place in homes across Scotland in the early hours of January 1. The first-footer must be out of the house before the clock strikes midnight, then cross the threshold to welcome in the new year, bringing gifts such as coal to lay on the fire, salt, bread and a wee bottle of whisky to toast the new year. To arrive empty-handed would be considered unlucky for the household.

WILDFOWL WATCH

The term 'wildfowl' refers to medium to large birds with rather long or very long necks, mostly short, broad bills, short legs and the front three toes joined by webs, such as ducks, geese and swans. These birds migrate to the UK in their masses for our relatively mild winters and easy-to-find food sources, only returning to their breeding grounds in spring. Head out to coastal areas and you'll find large flocks of geese, plus some of the rarer ducks including the pintail, goldeneye, long-tailed duck, red-breasted merganser and goosander. While it's common to feed wild fowl bread, this doesn't provide them with much nutritional value. Instead, try giving them grapes that have been deseeded and cut in half, cracked corn, oats and other grains, or peas and sweetcorn.

Walking in a winter

SISTERLY LOVE

Seven Sisters, Sussex

The Seven Sisters cliffs are some of Britain's most iconic (often doubling for the White Cliffs of Dover in films) and make for a wonderful wintery walk. Follow the South Downs Way from Birling Gap to Belle Tout Lighthouse (walking anti-clockwise will keep the winds at your back) and circle back to the Tiger Inn for atmospheric surroundings - oak beams, log fire and all of the classic cosy ingredients for a perfect winter's day. Try the bracing five-and-a-half miler to work up an appetite for a pub lunch.
www.beachyhead.org.uk

WALK THROUGH HISTORY

Bar Walls of York, Yorkshire

There are a whopping two miles of medieval city walls to wander along in York, and they look particularly dramatic in the stark winter light. They're the most complete and the longest of their kind in England, having survived attack from Vikings and Normans, and they are free to enjoy. Complete the route (with fab city views) in around two hours, or hop on and off to admire other local attractions such as botanical gardens or the minster. Warm up in one of the city's numerous cosy tea rooms afterwards.
www.yorkwalls.org.uk

WALK LIKE A ROYAL

Windsor Great Park, Surrey/Berkshire border

We can't promise that Snow Hill will be seasonally sprinkled in the white stuff, but we can guarantee you'll be walking through history - it's where Henry VIII is said to have waited for news of Anne Boleyn's execution. You'll find it at the end of Windsor Park's Long Walk - a pretty, tree-lined avenue that certainly feels regal - and capped with a statue of George III. The hill also offers fabulous views of the castle. For an eight-mile challenge, leave the park and head to the Runnymede memorials, before returning to Windsor along the Thames Path.
www.windsorgreatpark.co.uk

wonderland

PIC: NATIONAL TRUST

EYES TO THE SKIES

Box Hill, Surrey

The sparse landscapes of winter are ideal for honing your bird watching skills, and Box Hill is home to lots of kestrels, easy to identify thanks to their small size and distinctive hovering flight. Take an eight-mile circular walk that's challenging with steep slopes and some rough ground, but where the wildlife rewards are sure to be worth the effort. You can also see a folly which has an oak tree growing up through it (probably the result of a dropped acorn from a bird's beak), a Roman road and a lovely pub (the Running Horses) that's perfect for a lunch break.
www.nationaltrust.org.uk/box-hill

LAKE VIEWS

Clumber Park, Nottinghamshire

For an easy route that boasts lovely views and a variety of landscapes, try a two-mile jaunt through Clumber Park. Squirrel spotters should keep their eyes peeled, and the truly fortunate might spot jays or green woodpeckers. Clamber Clumber Bridge for views over the lake and chapel, before wandering through heathland and woodland. It's lovely year-round, but there's something satisfying about a stroll in cold weather followed by a steaming cuppa to make you feel worthy - and there are several cafes here to choose between, as well as a second-hand book shop to browse.
www.nationaltrust.org.uk/ clumber-park

CHILLS AND THRILLS

Holy Island, Northumberland

Only the brave will venture out on this atmospheric stretch of coastline - or should we say, ghostline? It's rumoured there are Viking spooks who wander the shore... Supernatural visitors aside, there's plenty to hold your attention on this six-mile circuit, including a ruined priory, Lindisfarne Castle and wildlife to spot including grey seals, dolphins and porpoises. Time your visit to coincide with the low tides, so you can cross the causeway - make sure to check the weather before you go.
www.lindisfarne.org.uk

Heavenly holly

Nothing says Christmas like the jewel-like red berries and glossy leaves of this winter wonder!

From a sprig on the mantlepiece to a wreath on the door, holly's spiky green leaves and gleaming red berries are a sign that festivities are on their way. Decorating the house with berry-laden branches snipped from the garden is a wonderful way to kick off seasonal celebrations.

A holly bush will earn its keep. Evergreen, it adds year-round structure, contrasting summer planting with its solid shape and standing crisply during the colder months adding rich green tones when much else has disappeared under the soil. It will put up with pollution from traffic and clips brilliantly, so a neatly clipped dome is an easy and striking choice for front gardens. Two holly lollipops in a pair of matching pots provide a warm welcome at the front door. It also works as a prickly leafed hedge to keep intruders out.

Plant a holly now and make the most of it this winter, indoors and out. English holly (Ilex aquifolium) is the one that often decorates our Christmas cards. It has the glossy pointed leaves and shiny red berries that are perfect to snip for a sprig on top of the Christmas pud. It's the best one for a traditional wreath or garland, or for weaving among tea lights on the table for Christmas lunch.

In the wild, it's a tall tree but, because it grows incredibly slowly, it works in a smaller garden.

For berries, you typically need two plants, a male and female, and only the female's fruit.

Pop your head over the fence to check if your neighbours have got one as hollies don't need to be in the same garden and you might make a match that way. If not, Holly 'JC Van Tol' is the only holly that will produce berries reliably without another plant close by.

PERFECT FOR A POT

Hollies grow very slowly so buy a plant that's close to the final size of lollipop you want. A standard tree will decorate your garden for years so give it the very best start. Choose a pot and stand the holly tree in it to see if the balance between the size of the tree and the size of the pot are right. They should be in proportion, ideally with the top of the lollipop similar in size to the pot. A small tree will struggle to fill a huge pot and the excess compost will turn sour. A pot that's too small won't allow the roots to grow, will need watering more often and may blow over in the wind.

Half fill the pot with John Innes No. 3. compost for mature plants. Tap the tree out of its container and tease out some of the roots. Position it in the hole in the compost, making sure the plant's stem is buried to the same depth as it was in the original pot. Backfill with more compost and firm down with your hands. Water the soil thoroughly with a full watering can.

THREE OF THE BEST HOLLIES FOR DECORATION

Ilex Aquifolium
The traditional bright red berried holly and our most common native hedging plant.

Ilex Aquifolium 'Bacciflava'
Enjoy its showy yellow berries and lots of them in autumn and winter.

Ilex Aquifolium 'Amber'
With orange berries it's great when snipped and paired with 'Bacciflava' for a wreath.

HOW TO GET MORE BERRIES

◆ Choose the right plant. Holly 'J C Van Tol' will always produce berries but lots of hollies need another holly bush nearby to make them berry up.

◆ Don't prune too often. Hollies grow very slowly, often hardly at all for the first two or three years after they're planted, so just snip off the branches you want to use for decoration. There's no need to neaten the plant so hold back with the secateurs.

◆ Water well, especially if your holly is in a pot. Dry roots make holly less likely to fruit.

Modern Gardens, hundreds of easy ideas, projects and fresh inspiration every month.

Santa's little helpers

These festive elves are the perfect project to make with the grandchildren!

YOU WILL NEED

**5 different felt colours: light
red, dark red, turquoise, moss
green and olive green
3 small pine cones
2.5cm (1in) wooden bead
Hot glue gun and glue stick
Black and red felt tip pens**

1 Trace the templates below
onto paper and use them to
cut out your felt hats, scarfs,
feet and gloves.

2 Fold the triangle felt hat pieces
in half and blanket stitch
the edge. Sew a mini bell
on the end.

3 Using the gun, glue the felt feet
on the bottom of the cones.

Yours tip: If your elves
don't stand up on their own,
cut out another foot shape out
in felt and glue on as an extra
layer to give them support.

4 Next glue the hats onto the
wooden balls. Draw two dots
for eyes and another dot for the
mouth.

5 Use the glue gun to stick each
wooden head to a pine cone
body. Tie the scarf in place and
glue down to keep secure.

6 Fringe the edges of the
scarf by snipping them with
scissors.

**Taken from LiaGriffith.
com. Become a member
for just £4 a month and get
access to more than 40 new
DIY projects a month.**

Gloves x 6
cut out three
pairs of gloves

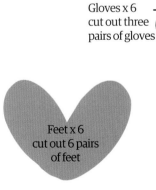

Feet x 6
cut out 6 pairs
of feet

Hat x3
Use a different colour
for each elf.

Scarf x3

Notable dates 2019

New Year's Day (Bank Holiday observed)	Tuesday January 1
Bank Holiday (Scotland)	Wednesday January 2
Epiphany	Sunday January 6
Burns' Night	Friday January 25
St David's Day	Friday March 1
Shrove Tuesday (Pancake Day)	Tuesday March 5
Ash Wednesday	Wednesday March 6
Chinese New Year (Pig)	Tuesday February 5
Valentine's Day	Thursday February 14
Commonwealth Day	Monday March 11
St Patrick's Day (Bank Holiday N. Ireland/Eire)	Sunday March 17
Mothering Sunday	Sunday March 31
British Summer Time begins (clocks go forward)	Sunday March 31
Palm Sunday	Sunday April 14
Maundy Thursday	Thursday April 18
First Day of Passover (Jewish Holiday)	Friday April 19
Good Friday (Bank Holiday)	Friday April 19
Easter Sunday	Sunday April 21
Easter Monday (Bank Holiday)	Monday April 22
St George's Day	Monday April 23
First Day of Ramadan (Islam)	Sunday May 5
May Day (Early May Bank Holiday)	Monday May 6
Ascension Day	Thursday May 30
Spring Bank Holiday	Monday May 27
Fathers' Day	Sunday June 16
Summer Solstice (Longest day)	Friday June 21
Armed Forces Day	Saturday June 29
American Independence Day	Thursday July 4
Battle of the Boyne (Holiday N. Ireland)	Friday July 12
St Swithun's Day	Monday July 15
Summer Bank Holiday (Scotland / Eire)	Monday August 5
Summer Bank Holiday	Monday August 26
Islamic New Year	Saturday August 31
Jewish New Year (Rosh Hashanah)	Sunday September 29
Trafalgar Day	Monday October 21
British Summer Time ends (clocks go back)	Sunday October 27
Hallowe'en	Thursday October 31
Diwali (Hindu Festival)	Sunday October 27
All Saints' Day	Friday November 1
Guy Fawkes' Night	Tuesday November 5
Remembrance Sunday	Sunday November 10
St Andrew's Day	Saturday November 30
First Sunday in Advent	Sunday December 1
Winter Solstice (Shortest day)	Saturday December 21
CHRISTMAS DAY	Wednesday December 25
BOXING DAY	Thursday December 26
New Year's Eve/Hogmanay	Tuesday December 31

THE YEAR AHEAD

30 SUNDAY

31 MONDAY

1 TUESDAY

2 WEDNESDAY

3 THURSDAY

4 FRIDAY

5 SATURDAY

Blast from the past

THE SEA FROZE OVER

I remember the severe winter of 1962/63. We were living in Hampshire and went on our motorcycle to spend Christmas with relations in Dorset. It started snowing on Boxing Day when we were halfway into our journey home. It was so bad that my husband had to remove his goggles to see where he was going along the dark country roads. When we reached home, we found the snow had frozen his eyebrows!

We were very relieved to get out of Dorset when we did. Most of the villages were cut off for weeks until bulldozers or snowploughs could reach them. Helicopters flew in supplies and feed for the cattle. Rivers froze over so people could skate and play games. Even the sea froze in Poole harbour so the postman was able to walk on it to deliver mail to Brownsea Island!

It was so cold that we did not see the ground again until March. Our house had no mod cons so drying the washing was difficult. If I pegged a sheet out it remained there for three days. We carried it in, frozen solid, black with smuts from the steam engines that ran along the bottom of the garden.
Pat Lowe, Basingstoke

Where did that come from?

'Break the ice'
Whether it's a funny joke or an interesting choice of chat, this phrase, meaning to relieve the tension, actually has marine beginnings. It stems from the fact there used to be small ships called 'icebreakers' which would rescue larger ships that had been caught in ice by breaking the solid ice and making a path through which the larger ship could escape.

Old-fashioned household tips

If you find your dentures a bit slippery to clean and worry about damaging them, fill the sink with water and place a flannel at the bottom of the sink. Should you accidentally drop your dentures in the sink, they will land on the wet flannel and not crack.

Animal magic

The loudest animal sound happens under the waves. It's a good job too, as the sperm whale's clicking call can reach up to 230 decibels. Normal conversation is around 50 decibels and a sound of 150 decibels is thought to be loud enough to burst a human's eardrums!

Do you remember?

Twin-tub washing machines

A god-send to all housewives, the twin-tub revolutionised the weekly washday when it arrived on the market in the Fifties. Its dual function of washing and spinning made much lighter work of laundry even if it did fill our kitchens with steam.

Recipe of the week

TRIO OF FISH PIE

Serves: 4 Prep: 15 mins Cook: 20 mins

500g (1lb 2oz) Charlotte potatoes, thinly sliced
25g (1oz) unsalted butter
25g (1oz) plain flour
300ml (½ pt) semi-skimmed milk
75g (3oz) light soft cheese
1 tsp salt
1 tsp wholegrain mustard
25g (1oz) pack chives, chopped
500g (1lb 2oz) diced mixed cod, salmon, cooked prawns

1 Preheat the oven to 200°C/400°F/Gas Mark 6.
2 Cook the potatoes in boiling water for 5 mins, drain.
3 Meanwhile, melt the butter in a medium saucepan and add the flour, cook for 30 secs. Gradually whisk in the milk and bring to the boil, stirring until thickened. Add soft cheese, salt, mustard and chives.
4 Stir the fish into the sauce and cook for 2-3 mins, transfer to an ovenproof serving dish. Top with the potatoes and season with black pepper. Bake for 20 mins until golden.
www.losalt.com

6 SUNDAY

7 MONDAY

8 TUESDAY

9 WEDNESDAY

10 THURSDAY

11 FRIDAY

12 SATURDAY

Blast from the past

'WE WILL CONNECT YOU'

I'm seated second from left in this photo taken when I was working on the manual telephone exchange at Codsall, near Wolverhampton. It was a small switchboard in the front room of a residential house with a large bay window.

There was a red public phone box in the front garden. Quite often customers would knock on the window asking for change or phone numbers. If they were strangers to the village they wanted to know how to use the phone as there was no dial. We told them: "Just lift the handset and we will connect you."

The advent of STD (Subscriber Trunk Dialling) meant the end of our switchboard. During 1965 a team of engineers arrived to prepare for the switchover to the new exchange in January 1966. It was timed precisely for one o'clock and the countdown was like the launch of a spaceship. There was a cacophony of bangs and breaking glass as debris hit the floor and ceiling. We watched as the switches, which were like dolls' eyes, flopped up and down, then twitched and stopped. All went quiet. Muriel who sat next to me said: "It's just like someone dying," with tears running down her cheeks.

Paddy Darby, Wolverhampton

Where did that come from?

'Bob's your uncle'

Said to end a simple set of instructions or when we've got the result we wanted, this saying comes from the time when British Prime Minister Lord Salisbury – whose first name was Robert, aka Bob – appointed his favourite nephew, Arthur Balfour to several political posts in the 1880s, setting him on the path to become Prime Minister after his uncle.

Old-fashioned household tips

Does your plastic chopping board slide about on the work surface when you're trying to use it? Try popping a damp piece of kitchen towel flat underneath the board to stop it from moving about.

Animal magic

Beavers' teeth never stop growing and to keep them in check they constantly gnaw wood. These rodent wood-whittlers are master dam-builders and the largest recorded beaver dam can be found in the Wood Buffalo National Park in Canada. At around 2790 feet in length, it can even be seen from space.

Do you remember?

Tupperware parties

For some, it was an excuse to have a natter with neighbours while earning a shilling or two. But Tupperware parties have since been considered an important part of women's liberation, allowing housewives a peek into the world of commerce by selling airtight storage containers to others.

Recipe of the week

BLACKBERRY CHIA AND LEMON PUDDING

Serves: 4 Prep: 25 mins Cook: 35-40 mins

Zest of 1 lemon
100g (4oz) caster sugar
100g (4oz) margarine
2 eggs
100g (4oz) self-raising flour
4 tsp chia seeds
150g (5oz) blackberries
1 tbsp cornflour
2 tbsp water
2 egg yolks
juice of 1 lemon
100g (4oz) puréed blackberries

1 Preheat oven to 180°C/350°F/Gas Mark 4. Brush 4, 200ml (7fl oz) metal pudding moulds with oil then line bases with a circle of baking paper.
2 Blitz the lemon zest with the sugar in a food processor. Add the marg and blitz again until smooth. Add the eggs and flour and mix until smooth. Stir in the chia seeds and blackberries.
3 Divide between pudding moulds. Cover each with a square of oiled foil then stand them in a roasting tin that is half filled with boiling water. Cover tin with foil and bake for 35-40 mins.
4 Make custard by mixing 1 tbsp cornflour with 2 tbsp water in a small pan. Mix in the egg yolks and when smooth, stir in lemon juice and puréed blackberries. Boil and stir until thick. Remove from heat and stir until smooth. Drizzle over cooked puds.

www.seasonalberries.co.uk

13 SUNDAY

14 MONDAY

15 TUESDAY

16 WEDNESDAY

17 THURSDAY

18 FRIDAY

19 SATURDAY

Blast from the past

POORLY LITTLE GIRL

I had more than my fair share of childhood illnesses, starting when I was just three years' old. My mother called me in from playing outside and took one look at me. The next instant the doctor came and I was in hospital. I had chickenpox, covered in spots from head to foot. My hair was chopped off and I was put in isolation for a month.

When I was four I had measles. Again I was put in isolation and after hospital I went to a convalescent home so I didn't see any of my family for three months. While I was away they moved from two rooms to a new house in Dagenham.

After this I suffered from impetigo and dermatitis. Aged nine, because I was pale and underweight I was sent to another convalescent home for ten months. Many of the other children there had TB. We slept in little chalets. In addition to sunlamp treatment I was given cod liver oil, malt and Parrish's food for invalids - yuk! Despite that, I caught everything going, including scabies.

Now that I'm getting on in years, I'm still pale but have put on weight and my health is fine.
Mrs A Ward, Sudbury

Where did that come from?

'Mad as a hatter'

It might sound barmy now, but back in the 19th Century, hat manufacturing involved a lot of mercury, which harmed the nervous system of the people who worked in this trade - known as 'hatters'. The mercury would make them tremble and insane, leading to this common phrase to mean someone is completely mad. Interestingly, mercury poisoning is still known today as mad hatter's disease.

Old-fashioned household tips

Want an easy way to cut a cake into even slices? Try using a piece of cotton or unscented dental floss. This also works well if you need to cut a home-baked cake into layers. Simply place cocktail sticks around the cake to use as a guide.

Animal magic

Elephants are the one mammal that can't jump. But, what they lack in athletic ability, they make up for in intelligence. Elephants' brains are structured in the same way as humans, apes and dolphins, indicating complex intelligence. They can show many emotions including joy, grief and even a sense of humour.

Do you remember?

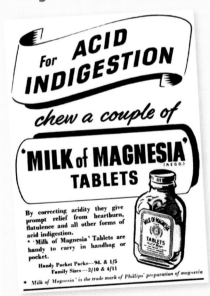

For ACID INDIGESTION chew a couple of 'MILK of MAGNESIA' TABLETS

By correcting acidity they give prompt relief from heartburn, flatulence and all other forms of acid indigestion.
* 'Milk of Magnesia' Tablets are handy to carry in handbag or pocket.
Handy Pocket Packs—9d. & 1/5
Family Sizes—2/10 & 4/11
* 'Milk of Magnesia' is the trade mark of Phillips' preparation of magnesia

Milk of Magnesia

Love it or hate it, our mums certainly enjoyed giving us this at even the faintest mention of a dicky tummy or heartburn. They told us it tasted like mints from the sweet shop, but we were never too sure.

Recipe of the week

PASTA CARBONARA

Serves: 4 Prep: 10 mins Cook: 8 mins

400g (14oz) spaghetti
250g (9oz) reduced-salt back bacon, roughly chopped
1 tbsp olive oil
1 garlic cloves, crushed
½ bunch spring onions, trimmed and chopped
4 large eggs
4 tbsp single cream
Salt and ground black pepper to taste
60g (2½oz) Parmigiano Reggiano, finely grated
A little parsley, chopped, to serve

1 Cook the spaghetti for 8 mins until al dente.
2 Fry the bacon in the olive oil until almost crisp, then add the garlic and spring onions and cook for 2 mins. Remove from the heat.
3 Beat together the eggs and cream with a little black pepper and set aside.
4 Drain the cooked pasta and return to the hot pan.
5 Stir in the bacon followed by the Parmigiano Reggiano.
6 Pour in the egg mixture, immediately stirring through the pasta - the heat from the pasta will cook the eggs to give a creamy sauce. Sprinkle with chopped parsley and serve immediately.
Aldi

20 SUNDAY

21 MONDAY

22 TUESDAY

23 WEDNESDAY

24 THURSDAY

25 FRIDAY

26 SATURDAY

Blast from the past

MY LOVELY MUM

This photo of my mum, Val, was taken around 1957 on the roof of the London factory where she had worked for two years since leaving school. Aged 17, she is wearing a fashionable dress which was black and white with a bright pink belt. She remembers feeling very trendy when she wore it. With her jet-black hair and trim figure, she was often complimented and told that she looked like Ava Gardner or Elizabeth Taylor. I agree, although I'm biased and think Mum is even lovelier than they were.

Mum was a war baby, born in 1940. She spent the first few years of her life sleeping in a drawer from a chest-of-drawers in the bomb shelter built in the garden by my granddad. Today Mum blames her rheumatism on those early days spent in a damp drawer!

Mum is still a fashionista. Although she is in her 70s she is still young at heart and an Abba fan - a real 'dancing queen'. Despite some health issues she has a lovely attitude to life and is a kind, caring person.

Debbie Isaac, via email

Where did that come from?

'Bite the bullet'

The theory goes that this saying for getting on with doing something unpleasant comes from when wounded soldiers in the First World War were being operated on. Without any anaesthetic available, they were encouraged to bite hard on a bullet to try to deal with the pain and protect them from biting their own tongues (ouch!).

Old-fashioned household tips

If you suspect a sink blockage might be caused by grease, pour baking soda as far down the plug hole as you can, and then pour in some vinegar. When it's stopped fizzing, pour down boiling water - this is much gentler solution than the corrosive chemicals you can buy and it's a lot cheaper!

Animal magic

A giant panda's diet consists of 99 per cent bamboo. As food choices go it's nutritionally quite poor, so they have to eat at least 12-38kg a day to meet their energy requirements. But they do branch out, with about 1% of their diet comprising other plants and even meat. While they are almost entirely vegetarian, pandas will sometimes hunt for pikas and other small rodents.

Do you remember?

Dansette players

All 'hip' teenagers had a Dansette on which to play their 'trendy' LPs from Cliff to The Beatles. Its portable size made it perfect for parties where we could dance into the night - or until our parents told us to keep the noise down.

Recipe of the week

GNOCCHI GRATIN WITH MEATBALLS AND MOZZARELLA

Serves: 4 Prep: 5 mins Cook: 20 mins

2 tsp olive oil
300g (10½oz) pack pork meatballs
350g (12oz) jar Italian Napoletana pasta sauce
500g (1lb 2oz) pack fresh potato gnocchi
125g (4½oz) pack mozzarella, drained
½ x 25g pack fresh basil, roughly torn

1 Heat the oil in a pan and fry the meatballs for 5-6 mins, until lightly browned. Stir in the pasta sauce. Cover and cook for 5 mins.
2 Meanwhile, cook the gnocchi according to pack instructions. Preheat the grill to a moderate temperature.
3 Drain the gnocchi and stir into the meatball mixture. Transfer to a heatproof dish then slice or tear the mozzarella into pieces and scatter over the top. Grill for 4-5 mins until the cheese has melted and is bubbling.
4 Garnish with basil and serve immediately with a fresh salad.

Waitrose

27 SUNDAY

28 MONDAY

29 TUESDAY

30 WEDNESDAY

31 THURSDAY

1 FRIDAY

2 SATURDAY

Blast from the past

SLEEPING BEAUTY

This is me with my sisters, Helen and Marion, in the Sixties (I am on the left). After leaving school I did a season as a redcoat at Butlin's in Bognor before becoming a sportswear sales consultant at Derry & Tom's department store in Kensington High Street.

Our buyer, Miss Payne, was an old-fashioned spinster who wore plaid suits and pinned-up hair. She was very fussy, but not really a dragon because she allowed me to come in to work at 9am instead of 8.45 because my journey from St Albans took an hour and a half.

On one particular day she mentioned to me that some of the directors would be visiting the store. When it was my lunch break I was feeling very tired so I thought I would sneak into the stock room for a little sleep to freshen up. I lay down behind the stock rails and didn't hear anything until there was a loud scream. Miss Payne had ushered the visiting VIPs in and she thought I was a dead body! Needless to say, it was very embarrassing for both of us. Luckily, I still kept my job. **Carolyne Martin, via email**

Where did that come from?

'Raining cats and dogs'

No one exactly knows where this rather bizarre 17th Century expression for heavy rain comes from. But it's most likely that it came about to describe the dead animals and other debris that would often be washed up in the constantly filthy streets after a heavy rainfall. It could alternatively come from a mishearing or hashing of the French word 'catadoupe' meaning waterfall.

Old-fashioned household tips

Smashed a glass? Don't worry! When clearing up broken glass from a hard floor surface use a damp or disposable cloth or a damp bar of soap to pick up all those small shards that could get stuck in your feet. Ouch!

Animal magic

Tiger stripes are completely unique to each individual, just like human fingerprints. They're the only cat species that are truly striped and even have stripes on their skin. Tigers are also one of the few members of the cat family that actually like to swim!

Do you remember?

School milk

It may have been slightly on the warm side and often had peculiar bits in the bottom, but nevertheless we loved our bottle of school milk. Introduced in 1906, free milk was said to help provide nutrition for those from poor families.

Recipe of the week

PORK WITH SAGE AND MARSALA SAUCE WITH POTATO AND PARSNIP MASH

Serves: 2 Prep: 15 mins Cook: 15 mins

1 large parsnip, diced
300g (10½oz) floury potatoes, diced
250g (9oz) pork fillet, sliced into 6
10g (½oz) sage
1 tbsp oil
100ml (4fl oz) Marsala wine
4 tbsp crème fraîche

1 Boil the parsnip and potato for 10-15 mins until tender, then drain.
2 Meanwhile, place the pork slices between 2 sheets of cling film and beat with a rolling pin until flattened. Season and place a large sage leaf on each piece.
3 Heat the oil in a frying pan and fry a further 4 whole sage leaves for a few seconds until crispy, drain and reserve.
4 Add the pork to the pan, sage side down first and fry for 2 mins each side. Add the Marsala wine and remaining sage, shredded and cook for 1-2 mins until reduced slightly.
5 Mash the parsnip and potatoes and stir in the crème fraîche and season to taste, serve with the pork and pour over the sauce.

www.lovefreshherbs.co.uk

3 SUNDAY

4 MONDAY

5 TUESDAY

6 WEDNESDAY

7 THURSDAY

8 FRIDAY

9 SATURDAY

Blast from the past

THE BIRTHDAY GIRL

My 21st birthday was in February 1987. To celebrate I had a party for my family and friends at the Three Kings Inn near our village of Shieldhill. It was a fabulous night with lots of lovely memories.

Singing telegrams were very popular at the time so my mum organised one for me. As I loved reading fairytales as a child and enjoyed romantic fiction, she asked the singing telegram to come as a frog then change into Prince Charming.

The company she approached didn't have an appropriate outfit, but they liked the idea and had one made specially for the occasion. The 'telegram' duly arrived wearing a frog suit, looking like a gigantic Kermit from The Muppets. My photo shows him in mid-transition from frog to prince. He then read out a poem to me. As you can see, I was a little taken aback.

Check out my big hair and white stilettos - very fashionable at the time. I loved my purple tafetta dress as it made me feel like a real princess.
Sharon Haston, Falkirk

Where did that come from?

'Three sheets to the wind'

In this case 'sheets' actually means the ropes with which a ship's sail is fastened. If, out of the four sheets necessary to hold a sail, one was not properly fastened - meaning there were only three 'sheets' left - a ship would become difficult to control against the wind and wander erratically, rather like the drunken state it now describes.

Old-fashioned household tips

A fab tip when cleaning up a grubby chamois rag or pair of leather gloves is to add a teaspoon of olive oil to the water. This will make them nice and soft and stop them going hard when they've dried out.

Animal magic

Chickens are nowhere near as bird-brained as often thought. They're in fact quite intelligent, with impressive memories and research has shown that chickens can even learn to count. They're also the closest living relative to the T. Rex!

Do you remember?

Green shield stamps

Given out by all the local shops as a way of rewarding customer loyalty, we got one stamp for every 6d spent and collected these in a little book. Once we had enough we could then excitedly pick a gift from the Green Shield Stamp glossy catalogue.

Recipe of the week

STICKY CLEMENTINE PUDDINGS

Serves: 8 Prep: 15 mins Cook: 30-35 mins

5 clementines
3 tbsp golden syrup
175g (6oz) butter
175g (6oz) golden caster sugar
3 eggs
85g (3oz) self-raising flour
85g (3oz) breadcrumbs
1tsp mixed spice
1 grated carrot
75g (2½ oz) sultanas

1 Preheat oven to 200°C/400°F/Gas Mark 6. Lightly butter 8x150ml (5floz) pudding moulds and 8 squares of foil.
2 Cut 8 thick slices from 2 clementines, grate the zest and squeeze the juice from another 3. Pour the golden syrup into the base of the moulds then sit a clementine slice in each.
3 Whisk the butter and sugar until pale then slowly whisk in the eggs. Stir in the flour, the zest and juice, breadcrumbs, mixed spice, grated carrot and sultanas.
4 Spoon into moulds, cover with foil, buttered-side down. Place in a roasting tin of boiling water halfway up side of dishes.
5 Bake for 30-35 mins until set. Serve with warmed custard.
Waitrose

10 SUNDAY

11 MONDAY

12 TUESDAY

13 WEDNESDAY

14 THURSDAY

15 FRIDAY

16 SATURDAY

Blast from the past

TRY, TRY AGAIN

I have always liked knitting and dressmaking and used to make skirts for myself as a teenager. When I got married at the age of 19 I had a lovely wedding dress made for me by a friend of my mother's. It was white satin and my five bridesmaids wore dresses made of blue brocade.

When I was 21 I had my first daughter and I thought I would make her a christening gown out of the train of my wedding dress. Unfortunately, it was my first attempt at making anything from a paper pattern and it didn't turn out to be as easy as I thought it would be. I ended up with no christening gown and no wedding dress.

When my daughters asked me what happened to my wedding dress I had to tell them the tale of my disastrous failure and how it had ended up in the rubbish bin!

I didn't give up on dressmaking, though, and went on to make my two girls some lovely dresses and trousers. The saying 'If at first you don't succeed, try, try again' really is true.
Mrs S R Beale, Walsall

Where did that come from?

'Eat humble pie'

In the 14th Century, the heart, liver and entrails of an animal were called the 'numbles' which eventually got shortened to 'umbles'. These would often be baked in pies - called 'umble pies' - which somewhere along the way changed to 'humble pie', which, with its connection to the word 'humble' came to mean accepting you're wrong or act apologetically.

Old-fashioned household tips

If you have children's toys or garden furniture that spend most of their life outside exposed to the elements, then the nuts and bolts will have a tendency to rust. To help stop this from happening, put a coat of Vaseline on and around each part.

Animal magic

Romance is far from dead in the penguin world. Gentoo Penguins know how to woo their ladies, not with a diamond, but with a pebble. Male Gentoo Penguins will go to great lengths to find the perfect pebble to give to their mate - much like choosing an engagement ring!

Do you remember?

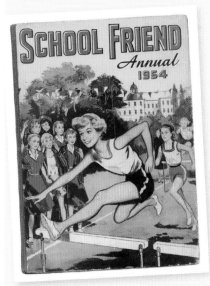

School Friend Annual

Published from 1926 to 1981, this was the yearbook all adventurous girls wanted for a bumper collection of stories, poems and general interest stories. Our favourite bits were gentle fashion features like 'Pretty up a plain dress in six gay ways'.

Recipe of the week

CREAMY TARRAGON CHICKEN

Serves: 4 Prep: 10 mins Cook: 25 mins

1 tbsp oil
4 chicken breasts
150ml (¼ pt) white wine
170ml (6fl oz) tub single cream
5 sprigs growing tarragon, roughly chopped

1 Fry the chicken in the oil for 15-20 mins, turning occasionally until golden and cooked through.
2 Remove the chicken from the pan and keep warm.
3 Add the wine to the pan and cook for 2 mins, then add the cream and tarragon and bring to the boil, stirring. Simmer for 1-2 mins.
4 Season with black pepper then pour over the chicken.
5 Serve with salad.
www.lovefreshherbs.co.uk

17 SUNDAY

18 MONDAY

19 TUESDAY

20 WEDNESDAY

21 THURSDAY

22 FRIDAY

23 SATURDAY

Blast from the past

THE GOOD OLD DAYS

Born in 1956, I was brought up with very little in the way of luxuries. Mum did our washing by hand and we had no vacuum cleaner, just a carpet sweeper. No fridge-freezer, just a pantry to keep things cool. It seems incredible that not many homes had bathrooms or inside toilets, just an old tin bath filled with water from the kettle and saucepans.

I remember our black-and-white television that had the epilogue on at the end of the evening. Afterwards, we watched the white dot slowly disappear from the screen as it went off air.

At my birthday parties all the food (cake, jelly, blancmange and ice-cream) and decorations were homemade. Party games such as Pin the Tail on the Donkey and Balloon Relay depended on skill and teamwork. My most well-loved present was a Barbie doll which is still famous more than 50 years later.

Although we had nothing, we didn't expect to be given much. All in all, we were happy!
Chris Wileman, Walsall

Where did that come from?

'Red herring'

This term for something misleading comes from the fact hunting dogs were generally trained to follow a scent by dragging the carcass of a salted herring (which was often red in colour) along the ground. There's also a thought that kind-hearted people created this false fishy trail so that the dogs would get confused and the real prey would escape.

Old-fashioned household tips

To keep your home smelling fresh, make you own pot-pourri from dried herbs or flower petals. Mint, sage, thyme, lemon verbena, bay leaves, rosemary and lemon-scented geranium are all perfect. Mix with cinnamon or cloves and a sprinkling of ground orris root for a preservative.

Animal magic

Sloths enjoy a doze, but not as much as you might think. In fact, they sleep less than ten hours a day. They're very slow though and it can take them up to a month to digest their mainly leaf-based diet, which is why they're so low in energy and appear sluggish.

Do you remember?

Camp coffee

It might not taste that much like the real thing, but we loved this coffee substitute anyway. Made of water, sugar, caffeine-free essence and chicory essence, it became the 'in' thing to drink in the mid-Seventies after the price of real coffee doubled because of shortages.

Recipe of the week

RASPBERRY AND APPLE FLAPJACKS

Serves: 10 Prep: 15 mins Cook: 20 mins

1 tbsp coconut oil
120g (4½ oz) apple sauce
80ml (3 floz) Alpro oat original drink (or use milk instead)
1½ tbsp honey
1 tbsp cinnamon
125g (4½ oz) oats
150g (5oz) raspberries

1 Pre-heat the oven to 180°C/350°F/Gas Mark 4 .
2 Grease a deep 15x15cm cake tin and set to one side. Melt the oil in a large pan. Mix with apple sauce until well-blended and smooth.
3 Add the oat original drink or milk, honey, cinnamon and oats and mix well.
4 Gently fold in raspberries. Pour the mixture into the tin and bake for 15-20 mins until golden brown. Remove from the oven and allow to cool before dividing the mixture into 10 equal pieces.
www.alpro.com

24 SUNDAY

25 MONDAY

26 TUESDAY

27 WEDNESDAY

28 THURSDAY

1 FRIDAY

2 SATURDAY

Blast from the past

STUDENT LIFE

This photo was taken in 1956 by a fellow student outside the halls of residence at the Diocesan Teacher Training College in Derby. I was trying to be sophisticated with my navy suede court shoes and permed hair. In those days I always wore skirts and blouses with flat shoes and never dreamed of wearing trousers as I do now. You always checked with a friend to make sure the seams on the back of your stockings were straight.

We were expected to change for dinner each night and were reprimanded by our teachers if our cardigan sleeves were pushed up our arms and reminded 'to act with the dignity of the profession we had chosen to enter'.

I had gone to the all-girls college after leaving Skegness Grammar School and was really quite naïve. We signed in each night and had a mentor, a second-year student, to show us around during the first few weeks. As I was from a large family my education and board were free.

I remember my two years there with affection; I made some lifelong friends and had a very good preparation for a career in teaching.
Audrey Chatterton, Spilsby

Where did that come from?

'Chip on your shoulder'

There was a time when Royal Navy dockyard workers were allowed to take their timber home. But when the Navy realised this was costing money, they changed the rules so workers could only carry the wood home with their hands, not on their shoulders, meaning they left work with less wood and more resentment, building up a grudge, which is the meaning of this phrase today.

Old-fashioned household tips

Removing a splinter in your hand can be painful. Carefully fill a wide-mouthed bottle with hot water nearly to the brim and press the affected part of hand tightly to the mouth of the bottle. The suction will pull down the flesh, and the steam will draw out the splinter.

Animal magic

Our furry feline friends have an incredible 32 muscles in each ear! They can rotate them 180 degrees and have better hearing than dogs. Each ear canal is filled with fluid, which helps them keep their balance and in theory ensures they always land on their feet!

Do you remember?

Transistor radios

From our humble teenage bedrooms, transistor radios were the means by which we escaped to the wild world of pop music. Handily, they were tiny enough to hide under pillows, meaning Mum never knew we were listening to John Peel and Tony Blackburn all night.

Recipe of the week

VEGGIE SPAGHETTI BOLOGNESE

Serves: 4 Prep: 15 mins Cook: 30 mins

180g (6oz) dried puy lentils
1 tbsp oil
1 clove garlic, chopped
1 onion, chopped
2 carrots, diced
2 sticks celery, diced
50ml (2fl oz) red wine
400g (14oz) can chopped tomatoes
1 tbsp tomato purée
2 tsp dried oregano
1 tsp LoSalt
300g (10½oz) wholewheat spaghetti

1 Cook the lentils in boiling water for 20 mins then drain.
2 Meanwhile, heat the oil in a saucepan and fry the garlic, onion, carrots and celery for 5 mins. Add the red wine and cook until reduced by half. Add the tomatoes, purée, oregano and LoSalt.
3 Half fill the tomato can with water and add to the pan.
4 Add the lentils and bring to the boil, simmer for 10 mins until lentils are tender.
5 Cook the spaghetti in boiling water for 10 mins or until tender, drain and serve with the bolognese.
losalt.com

3 SUNDAY

4 MONDAY

5 TUESDAY

6 WEDNESDAY

7 THURSDAY

8 FRIDAY

9 SATURDAY

Blast from the past

FRIENDS IN HARMONY

Here I am having fun with some joke spectacles and my dear friend Ayshe Sawkins (that's me on the left). We have been friends since we were 11 years' old when we attended Winchmore School in north London.

We both studied music and in 1976, when we were 14, we were founder members of the Bella Cora choir. We are still singing together in the same choir after all these years. For a while we both played in the Southgate symphony orchestra – Ayshe is a very good flautist and I used to play the French horn.

She also celebrated with me when I had been 25 years in my job and was my 'taxi' so that I could have a celebratory drink. As you can tell from the photo, we so enjoy each other's company and every year we take a trip to Cardiff together to visit another old friend from our schooldays.

Ayshe is married with two sons in their 20s. I have two daughters and when my grandson, Thomas, was born she came straight round with a blanket that she had knitted and a crocheted picture for him.
Hilary Biggs, Enfield

Where did that come from?
'Kick the bucket'
This byword for dying has an unsurprisingly morbid history, deriving from the idea that when people hanged, they would literally stand on a bucket that was kicked from underneath them, with a noose around their neck. Alternative suggestions are that in the 1500s 'bucket' meant a beam on which a slaughtered animal was hung, where they would struggle and literally kick the 'bucket'.

Old-fashioned household tips

The tops of kitchen cupboards, often get covered in grease and dust and can be really tough to clean. So the next time you clean up top, lay a sheet of greaseproof paper across the top of them. The next time you have a thorough clean, simply remove the dirty paper, wipe over the tops and replace the paper.

Animal magic

Baby names in the animal world are not always simple. Baby rabbits are called kittens, a baby antelope is called a calf and a baby bat is called a pup! A baby partridge is called a cheeper and a baby porcupine is a porcupette.

Do you remember?

Pea soupers

A dense kind of fog that choked up the streets, especially in the capital, pea soupers were common in Fifties Britain. During the worst one in 1952, fog was so thick you could only see a couple of yards ahead and 12,000 people sadly died.

Recipe of the week

YOGURT PANCAKES

Serves: 4 Prep:10 mins Cook: 4 mins

1 egg, beaten
150g (5oz) Greek-style yogurt
175ml (6floz) milk
1 tbsp melted butter, plus extra to grease
1 tsp caster sugar
½ tsp salt
150g (5oz) wholemeal flour
To serve:
20g (¾ oz) blueberries
20g (¾ oz) raspberries
Runny honey, to drizzle

1 Whisk the egg, yogurt, milk and melted butter together.
2 In a separate bowl, combine the sugar, salt and flour. Add the yogurt mixture to the dry ingredients and beat until smooth.
3 Lightly grease a frying pan and warm on a medium heat. Use 2 tbsp batter for each pancake and cook for 2 mins each side until golden brown.
4 Serve 2 pancakes each, with berries and runny honey.
Lakeland

10 SUNDAY

11 MONDAY

12 TUESDAY

13 WEDNESDAY

14 THURSDAY

15 FRIDAY

16 SATURDAY

Blast from the past

BEAUTY AND BRAINS

My mother, Jean, had a fascinating life. She combined film-star good looks with brains and bravery. The daughter of a British doctor who undertook refugee relief work abroad in the Twenties, she spoke several languages fluently including Greek, French, German, Italian and, naturally, English.

Eventually my mother and her parents settled in Greece, a country they adored. My grandfather assumed the reins of his family's export business and travelled extensively. When the Second World War broke out he was abroad and unable to return to Greece. The family were not reunited until after the war. In the meantime, my mother and grandmother lived under German occupation. They risked their lives helping allied soldiers and Jewish people to escape the enemy. In recognition of their bravery, my grandmother received a certificate from Field Marshall Alexander.

After the war, my mother used her linguistic skills to help refugees through her work as a translator for the United Nations. She was a positive influence on my life and taught me that courage and kindness have a more enduring impact than beauty.
Charmaine Fletcher, via email

Where did that come from?

'Paint the town red'

In 1837 the mischief-maker the Marquis of Waterford led friends on a night of drinking through Melton Mowbray. The bender culminated in lots of vandalism including painting several homes and a statue with red paint. While the Marquis and friends later paid for their damage, this is likely to be the origin for this shorthand saying for a wild night out.

Old-fashioned household tips

To test your eggs for freshness, pop it in a bowl of water. If the egg lays on its side at the bottom it's fresh, if it stands upright on the bottom it's good but eat it soon or hardboil. If it floats to the top – it's past its best, do not eat.

Animal magic

An average dog understands a vocabulary of around 250 words - far more than just sit and stay! Topping the intelligence stakes is the Border Collie and a survey found that 59 per cent could shake paws and even more impressively 24 per cent had learnt to open doors.

Do you remember?

Spangles

They ruined our teeth and left us destitute of pocket money, but Spangles were worth it. The highlight of any good sweet shop from the Fifties to the Eighties they came in a striped, brightly coloured paper tube and had different fruity flavours.

Recipe of the week

CHICKEN CASSEROLE

Serves: 3 Prep: 15 mins Cook: 30 mins

1 tsp olive oil
6 chicken thigh fillets
2-3 cloves garlic, finely sliced
400g (14oz) trimmed leeks, thinly sliced
400g (14oz) can haricot beans, drained and rinsed
3-4 sprigs fresh thyme
1 fresh bay leaf
150ml (¼ pt) dry white wine or chicken stock

1 Heat oil in a non-stick pan and cook the chicken over a high heat until brown. Drain on kitchen paper and keep warm.
2 Add the garlic and leeks to the pan and cook over a low heat for 3-4 mins until softened but not browned.
3 Add the beans, thyme, bay leaf and wine or stock and simmer for a further 4 mins.
4 Arrange the chicken thighs on top of the beans, cover the pan and cook over a low heat for 15-20 mins until the chicken is cooked through.

Waitrose

17 SUNDAY

18 MONDAY

19 TUESDAY

20 WEDNESDAY

21 THURSDAY

22 FRIDAY

23 SATURDAY

Blast from the past

MY FAIRYTALE CASTLE

I was 12 when I fell in love with this castle in the film Chitty Chitty Bang Bang. It inspired the castle that Walt Disney used in Sleeping Beauty.

Most people think it is a fictional place, but my husband Pete found the location of Castle Neuschwanstein and booked a holiday there for my 40th birthday. To reach it we flew to Munich followed by a three-hour train journey to Füssen from where we took a taxi to the village of Hohenschwangau. When we arrived I went out onto the balcony, looked up at 'my castle' and cried!

During our five days there we visited the castle every day and bought every souvenir we could find. We even took a cable car up the mountain so that we could view it from above. This photo of us both was taken on the Marienbrucke Bridge which (so the story goes) Queen Mary had built because she was fed up with King Ludwig coming home late for dinner after hunting trips.

Visitors can book a horse and carriage if they don't fancy the steep climb up to the castle – but it is well worth the effort.

Bren Morris, St Albans

Where did that come from?

'Crocodile tears'

A display of superficial upset, this saying actually comes from the medieval belief that crocodiles really did shed tears of sadness. It's thought they did this when they killed and consumed their prey (which sounds somewhat two-faced if you ask us). The phrase first appeared in a 14th Century book and was later popularised in the works of Shakespeare.

Old-fashioned household tips

Want a natural stain remover? White vinegar is a natural alternative for many household chemicals. It contains acetic acid, so ½ cup in your wash will brighten, whiten and soften your laundry as well as getting rid of any odour without harming the fabric.

Animal magic

A sea otter is one of the few mammals that uses its paws. One of the smallest marine animals, it is actually part of the weasel family. Rather adorably, to stop them drifting apart when floating in water sea otters often hold paws while they sleep.

Do you remember?

Trolls

The must-have fad of the Sixties and Seventies, trolls were crazy-looking things with wild hair, originally created in 1959 by a Danish woodcutter who carved the doll from his imagination when he couldn't afford a Christmas present for his daughter.

Recipe of the week

BRAISED SAUSAGES IN LEEK GRAVY

Serves: 4 Prep: 10 mins Cook: 20 mins

1 tbsp oil
8 pork sausages
500g (1lb 2oz) leeks, sliced
25g (1oz) plain flour
450ml (¾ oz) beef stock
1 tbsp Worcestershire sauce
1 tbsp wholegrain mustard

1 Preheat the oven to 200°C/400°F/Gas Mark 6.
2 Heat the oil in a large frying pan and fry the sausages for 5 mins to brown, transfer to an ovenproof casserole dish.
3 Add the leeks to the pan and fry for 2 mins, stir in the flour and cook for 30 seconds before gradually blending in the stock, Worcestershire sauce and mustard.
4 Bring to the boil, stirring and pour over the sausages. Cover and bake for 20 mins or until cooked through.
Discover Great Veg

24 SUNDAY

25 MONDAY

26 TUESDAY

27 WEDNESDAY

28 THURSDAY

29 FRIDAY

30 SATURDAY

Blast from the past

TREASURED THIMBLE

I still have the thimble that belonged to my grandmother. Using it when I sew brings back memories of her. She left school aged 14 and was married two months before her 18th birthday. She wore an emerald green dress - a white dress was considered a waste because it could never be worn again. Her first child was born when she was 19 and she went on to have a large family; my mother was her youngest. Later on, her father came to live with her so she had three adults and eight children to care for.

In spite of a life of hard work she always had a wonderful sense of humour and could cope with whatever her grandchildren got up to. When I was six, I remember one wet afternoon when I was allowed to brush her hair as she fell asleep in the armchair. Her hair was grey by then and I made as many fine little plaits as I could manage. It took her a long time to undo them all!

I loved to visit her, especially when I was allowed to stay the night and share her bed which seemed vast to a small child.

Dorrie Pearton, London

Where did that come from?

'Rub someone up the wrong way'

Meaning to annoy someone, this phrase may come from early Americans who would ask servants to rub their oak floorboards 'the right way' - with a wet cloth and then a dry one. Doing it the 'wrong way' would cause streaks and annoy them. Another suggestion is that it comes from cats which - as all feline fans know - hate being stroked in the 'wrong' direction.

Old-fashioned household tips

If you've bought candles that are slightly too big in diameter for the holder, rather than carve chunks off, which can be messy and leave the candles unstable, soften the wax by soaking the candle end in hot water, then gently push them into the holder.

Animal magic

A lion's roar can be heard as far as five miles away, which makes it the loudest of all the cat species. The roar is used to call other lions as well as claiming territory and it needs to be loud as a pride's territory can reach as far as 100 square miles.

Do you remember?

Hostess trolleys

To be the hostess with the mostest - and the epitome of the Seventies housewife - you had to have a hostess trolley, complete with hot plates and Pyrex dishes. They were ideal for fancy dinner parties and are now seeing a surprising return to the high street.

Recipe of the week

CINNAMON CHOCOLATE TRUFFLES

Makes: 30 Prep: 10 mins Cook: 10 mins (+ 4 hours chilling)

280g (10oz) good-quality dark chocolate
284ml (½ pt) double cream
50g (2oz) unsalted butter
1 tsp cinnamon extract
Cocoa powder and cinnamon sugar to coat

1 Chop the chocolate and place into a large bowl. Put the cream and butter into a saucepan and heat gently until the butter melts and mixture is just simmering.
2 Remove from heat, pour over the chocolate and stir until smooth. Add the cinnamon extract, allow the mixture to cool, then chill for 4 hours.
3 Shape the truffles using a piping bag or melon baller dipped in hot water. Place onto greaseproof paper.
4 Coat immediately after shaping; place a little cocoa powder and cinnamon sugar into a bowl, and gently roll the truffles until coated.
Lakeland

30 SUNDAY

1 MONDAY

2 TUESDAY

3 WEDNESDAY

4 THURSDAY

5 FRIDAY

6 SATURDAY

Blast from the past
ALL THROUGH THE YEARS

This photo of me with my best friend Margaret was taken when we were about 15 years old (I am on the right). We were in the same class at infants' school in Portsmouth in 1952. She lived in the next road to me so we walked to and from school together. Later we moved on to the same junior school, then secondary school. We played together at break times and shared the same friends.

As teenagers we went on dates together with various boyfriends and were bridesmaids at each other's weddings. We both gave birth to our first babies in the same year. Margaret and her husband spent some time in Spain running a bar. For 23 years my husband and I ran pubs in different parts of the country, but we always kept in touch. Wherever we lived we spent weekends and holidays at each other's houses when we could.

Now we all have grandchildren, but the four of us still meet up several times a year to celebrate birthdays and special days together. After 66 years we still enjoy each other's company and have never had a row.
Valerie Reilly, Reading

Where did that come from?
'To rest on your laurels'

This dates back to ancient Greek athletes who were awarded a crown of laurel leaves – symbolising status and achievement – when they won. These celebrated Greeks – called 'laureates' – could literally 'rest on their laurels' by basking in the glory of their past achievements. Only later in the 1800s would this acquire a negative connotation for someone who is overly satisfied with past victories.

Old-fashioned household tips

A top-heavy ornamental vase can have a tendency to fall over and break easily if knocked. A simple solution to this is to partially fill it with sand, this will make it heavier and help to keep the base stable.

Animal magic

The orca, or killer whale as it's known, is actually the largest species in the dolphin family. Long ago sailors would call the orca a whale killer, after seeing how it would sometimes hunt whales. Over the years this was altered to killer whale.

Do you remember?

Brasso

We can still remember the distinct smell when Mum or Dad decided it was time to Brasso all the door knobs in sight. First made in Britain in 1921 and still on shelves today, the metal polish shines up brass, copper, chrome or stainless steel a treat.

Recipe of the week

TAGLIATELLE WITH BROCCOLI, THYME AND MELTING CHEESE SAUCE

Serves: 4 Prep: 5 mins Cook: 10 mins

400g (14oz) dried tagliatelle pasta
200g (7oz) pack Tenderstem broccoli
250ml (½ pt) crème fraîche
200g (7oz) Tallegio cheese or brie, sliced
200g (7oz) Parmesan cheese, grated
2 cloves garlic, crushed
Small handful, chopped fresh thyme

1 Cook the tagliatelle according to packet instructions.
2 Meanwhile, cut the florets off the broccoli and slice the stems into chunks. Steam or boil for about 3 mins until tender.
3 While the pasta and broccoli are cooking, make the sauce by placing the crème fraîche, Tallegio (or brie) and Parmesan in a pan over a very low heat with the crushed garlic.
4 Add a small handful of chopped fresh thyme (oregano and marjoram would also work well) and heat everything gently, stirring to mix the melting cheese, adding a grind of fresh black pepper.
5 Once the sauce is ready pour it over the cooked pasta and broccoli and serve in deep bowls sprinkled with extra Parmesan and a good drizzle of extra-virgin olive oil.

www.tenderstem.co.uk

7 SUNDAY

8 MONDAY

9 TUESDAY

10 WEDNESDAY

11 THURSDAY

12 FRIDAY

13 SATURDAY

Blast from the past

AN EASTER TRADITION

It is a tradition in my home town of Horwich to climb a local hill called Rivington Pike at Easter time. This photo was taken on Good Friday 1958 when I was ten years' old. I am in the group on the left of the picture with my mum and dad and Mum's friend, Gladys. Gladys' daughter is holding the camera and I think Gladys' husband took this photo.

I don't know when this tradition started, but certainly for as long as my mother could remember (she was born in 1915).

In fact, my brother and I had already done the climb earlier in the day. In the Fifties, the churches in Horwich used to have a service at the top of the Pike at eight o'clock on Good Friday morning. Then we used to go back down to Sunday School for breakfast. In the afternoon, Gladys and her family came by bus from nearby Wigan and we all walked up the Pike then back to our house for tea.

People still go 'up the Pike' on Good Friday, but they are dressed rather differently these days!
Cynthia Pearcy, Bolton

Where did that come from?
'To bury the hatchet'
Meaning to stop a conflict and make peace, this dates back to early North America. When the Puritans were in conflict with the Native Americans and trying to negotiate for peace, the Native Americans would try to bury all of their weapons including knives, clubs, tomahawks and hatchets – a sharp, bladed tool to make them inaccessible for them to use.

Old-fashioned household tips

Decorating can be a messy affair and no matter how tidy you try to be, paint always seems to end up on the brush handle. Keep your brushes clean by cutting a hole in a piece of cardboard slightly smaller than your paint brush and force the paint brush through – no more sticky handles.

Animal magic

The platypus may look cute and cuddly, but actually it is one of the few venomous mammals, with a venom-secreting gland on the back of each hind leg. While it isn't deadly to humans, it would certainly make you feel very unwell!

Do you remember?

Dinky toys

These are serious collectibles today but in the Fifties and Sixties they were the toys our brothers craved. Made by Meccano, they were among the most popular Die-cast vehicles ever created and came in all kinds of models from Morris Pick Ups to Ford Prefects.

Recipe of the week

SCRAMBLED EGGS AND AVOCADO ON SEEDED TOAST

Serves: 2 Prep: 5 mins Cook: 5 mins

2 tbsp skimmed milk
3 free-range eggs, beaten
1 tsp finely grated parmigiano reggiano
2 medium slices seeded bread, toasted
1 baby avocado, skinned, stoned and diced
2 tsp snipped chives

1 Pour the milk into a small, non-stick saucepan and warm gently.
2 Add the eggs and parmigiano reggiano and cook for 3-5 mins, stirring continually until set and creamy.
3 Spoon the eggs on top of the toast, scatter over the avocado, sprinkle with chives and serve.

Waitrose

14 SUNDAY

15 MONDAY

16 TUESDAY

17 WEDNESDAY

18 THURSDAY

19 FRIDAY

20 SATURDAY

Blast from the past

OUR PRECIOUS FIRSTBORN

This photo reminds me of a very special day in my life – when I became a grandma for the first time. Although this was a happy occasion, it had been tinged with some very worrying moments. My daughter-in-law had pre-eclampsia and was really poorly when she still had five weeks to go. Under the circumstances it was decided to carry out a Caesarean section. My son was in a terrible state and rang me late at night in tears. We were living in Devon at that time and they were in Bedfordshire – it was hard being so many miles away.

About seven in the morning I rang the hospital and was told that she had improved which put my mind at rest. Getting the phone call from son saying, "Hello, Mum, you have a granddaughter" was unforgettable. It was made even more special by the fact that it was also my husband's birthday. We both sat on the bed and cried!

Since then we have had six more grandchildren, two more girls and four boys. They have all grown up into very special individuals and made us very proud grandparents, but that first time always stands out in our memory.

Sue Stevenson, Chard

Where did that come from?

'To turn a blind eye'

To ignore situations, facts or reality, this saying comes from a British Naval hero called Admiral Horatio Nelson who had one blind eye. Once, when British forces signalled to him to stop attacking a fleet of Danish ships, he held up a telescope to his blind eye and said 'I do not see the signal'. He attacked anyway and was later victorious.

Old-fashioned household tips

Lighting a barbecue or campfire with matches in a breeze can be difficult. Using a knife, cut some thin shavings into the top of the matchstick, just under the head. When you light the match, the curled shavings give the match increased surface area to make the flame stronger.

Animal magic

Although there are many similarities between rabbits and hares, the first few days of their lives are very different. Baby rabbits are born hairless and blind and spend their early day in a cosy, fur-lined nest. Hares on the other hand, are born with hair, with their eyes open and are able to run within an hour.

Do you remember?

Sindy doll

Launched in 1963, Sindy had everything a Sixties teen could want, with a Mary Quant-style wardrobe and a cool boyfriend called Paul. She was the 'girl you love to dress' so the adverts told us and was at times even more popular than Barbie in the UK.

Recipe of the week

PARSLEY SALSA VERDE WITH LAMB

Serves: 4 Prep: 10 mins Cook: 10 mins

2 tbsp extra-virgin olive oil
Zest and juice of 1 lemon
3 tbsp chopped fresh parsley
1 tbsp chopped fresh chives
1 tbsp chopped fresh thyme
1 tbsp capers, roughly chopped
4 lamb leg steaks

1 To make the salsa verde mix together the oil, lemon zest and juice, fresh herbs and capers. Season well and chill.
2 Pan-fry the leg steaks for 4-6 mins or until cooked to your liking.
3 Top the lamb with salsa verde and serve with new potatoes tossed with a little butter and chopped fresh parsley.

www.lovefreshherbs.co.uk

21 SUNDAY

22 MONDAY

23 TUESDAY

24 WEDNESDAY

25 THURSDAY

26 FRIDAY

27 SATURDAY

Blast from the past

MY ADOPTED MUM

I will always treasure this lovely photo of myself and my best friend, Joan, celebrating her 89th birthday. Sadly, she did not quite make it to her 90th. I was so lucky to have enjoyed her friendship for more than 11 years.

As I had lost my own mother, I adopted Joan in a way as a replacement. She was a widow without any living relatives of her own. She also acted as a grandmother to my daughter. We both loved her very much.

Joan was born way back in the Twenties and she enthralled me with stories from the past. She was worried that when she died no-one would want to keep her photographs, but I assured her that was not so and now I have a large album containing all her pictures.

We had such fun going out shopping and visiting cafés, where she would read out all the items on the menu but always ordered the same meal of ham, egg and chips. She had a great sense of humour. I learned so much from her - she was an expert on household budgets.

I miss her sparkling personality and wonderful smile, but she will always have a place in my heart.

Angela Patchett, Fleetwood

Where did that come from?

'Saved by the bell'

This came not from the Nineties' sitcom of the same name but from boxing slang in the late 19th Century. When a boxer is in danger of losing a bout they can be saved from defeat by a bell that marks the end of the round. Since then it's been synonymous with something that's rescued from a dire outcome by a timely occurrence.

Old-fashioned household tips

If you have important documents or cash you'd like to keep in a safe place for a short time, put it in an envelope and using a drawing pin, tack the envelope to the back of a drawer. Just write a little note to remind yourself it's there!

Animal magic

The Wood Frog is one of the few animals that can partly freeze and survive. When the temperature drops, its organs stop and as much as 65 per cent of the water in its body can freeze. It can stay this way for two to three months, before literally thawing out!

Do you remember?

Fondue parties

The Swiss had held gatherings around pots of sticky cheese for decades before, in the Seventies, we suddenly decided we'd do the same in Britain. Overnight we started buying up fondue sets and inviting guests round to poke bread and nibbles into melted cheese.

Recipe of the week

PLUM BAKEWELL

Serves: 8 Prep: 15 mins Cook: 30 mins

Ready-made tart base
2 tbsp raspberry jam
2 eggs
400g (14oz) caster sugar
20g (¾oz) almonds
1 tsp vanilla extract
zest of half a lemon
8 plums, pitted and halved
handful of flaked almonds
Icing sugar

1 Preheat the oven to 180°C/350°F/Gas Mark 4. Put a 21cm butter pastry tart onto a baking sheet and spoon on the jam.
2 Beat together the eggs, sugar, almonds, vanilla extract and the zest of half a lemon.
3 Spoon into the tart case and spread it out over the jam. Place the plums on top. Sprinkle with flaked almonds and bake in the oven for 25-30 mins, until the filling is set and golden. Cool for about 20 mins, then serve, sprinkling with icing sugar.

beautifulcountrybeautifulfruit.com

28 SUNDAY

29 MONDAY

30 TUESDAY

1 WEDNESDAY

2 THURSDAY

3 FRIDAY

4 SATURDAY

Blast from the past

LIVING THE DREAM

It was a dream come true! I couldn't believe that I was actually standing outside The Alamo with a camera in my hand. How I came to be there was a story that started back in 1942, in the darkest days of the Second World War. That was when I started writing to my penpal, Mary Alice from Sweetwater in Texas. We were both 11 years old.

Incredibly, 37 years later I found myself 'living the dream' in Sweetwater. Everything about Texas seemed larger than life. Even the motor home that Mary Alice shared with her husband, Earl, seemed bigger than my bungalow back home on Tyneside.

First on my list of things to see was The Alamo, the site of the famous battle where Davy Crockett and Jim Bowie fought. Mary Alice knew all about my passion for cowboy films and stories of the Deep South and the American Civil War so we also visited the ante bellum houses where the owners dressed in the style of Gone with the Wind.

I also learned why cowboy boots and Stetsons were still worn by my friends - the boots to ward off rattlesnakes and the hats as protection from the blazing sun.
Pat Berkshire, Hexham

Where did that come from?
'Get the sack'

The slang term for getting fired originates from French tradesmen who would always own their own tools and take them in a bag also known as a 'sack'. So that meant if they were dismissed from employment they had to take their 'sack' of tools with them. The first use of the phrase in English was in Charles Westmacott's The English Spy in 1825.

Old-fashioned household tips

The air in an egg can cause the shell to crack during the boiling process. Keep your eggs at room temperature and add vinegar to the water to prevent this from happening. To peel them easily, tap both ends of the egg on a sheet of kitchen towel on a hard surface and press lightly while rolling.

Animal magic

The swift spends most of its life in the air, so it's no surprise that in level flight they are the fastest of all birds. They do not perch or walk and do most things on the wing including sleeping and mating! The only time they land is to nest and raise their young.

Do you remember?

Have you remembered your –

Reckitt's BAG BLUE READY FOR USE

Reckitt's blue

Before modern laundry detergents, Reckitt's little blue bags were what kept our whites truly white. Sold as penny cubes to be wrapped in flannel or muslin, or ready-bagged, they were made of synthetic ultramarine and baking soda and sometimes known as Dolly Bags or Laundry Blue.

Recipe of the week

TUSCAN SAUSAGE AND WHITE BEAN STEW

Serves: 4 Prep: 10 mins Cook: 30 mins

1 onion, chopped
1 tbsp olive oil
2 garlic cloves
2 carrots, diced
4 pork sausages, sliced
500ml (1pt) fresh chicken stock
500g (1lb 2oz) cherry tomatoes, halved
400g (14oz) can cannellini beans, drained and rinsed
25g (1oz) flat-leaf parsley, leaves and stalks separated and chopped
200g (7oz) cavolo nero cabbage, tough stems discarded, leaves roughly chopped

1 Sauté the onions in the oil until they begin to soften. Finely chop the garlic and add to the pan along with the carrots, cook for 2 mins.
2 Add the sausage and cook for 5 mins, stirring occasionally, until just turning golden.
3 Tip in the stock, tomatoes, beans, parsley stalks and 500ml water. Bring to the boil, then simmer gently for 15 mins. Add the cavolo nero and simmer for another 5 mins. Season, stir the parsley leaves through and serve.

Waitrose

5 SUNDAY

6 MONDAY

7 TUESDAY

8 WEDNESDAY

9 THURSDAY

10 FRIDAY

11 SATURDAY

Blast from the past

FATHER OF THE BRIDE

This photo taken at my wedding is very special to me because it is a rare photo of my father. He was a very shy, quiet man who hated having his photo taken and didn't like socialising. He knew that the bride's father should speak at the reception and made himself ill worrying about this. I promised him that he need not make a speech and, although he was nervous throughout, I think he did enjoy the day.

The suit he is wearing is the same one that he himself had been married in and it had been carefully looked after. The only other photo I ever had of my father was one of him in his 'leathers'. When he was a young man he was a keen motorcyclist. He owned a Norton motorbike on which he had a serious accident that resulted in him losing the sight in his right eye. After this my mum insisted that he had a sidecar attached to his bike. I went on many trips with my father and found it exciting sitting in the green sidecar. I was heartbroken when that photo went missing after I moved house.　**Hazel Anderson, Leeds**

Where did that come from?
'Frog in the throat'
We've all said this when we've got sudden tickle but this American phrase comes from the fact a hoarse person sounds croaky like a frog. The expression must have been in popular use by 1894 when it was used in an advertisement as the name of a medicine for sore throats where it claimed 'Frog in the Throat' will cure hoarseness for only ten cents a box (what a bargain!)

Old-fashioned household tips

Protect your canvas summer shoes from an unexpected shower and puddles by giving them an even coating of beeswax. Melt some wax in a pan and work it into your shoes with a clean paintbrush paying attention to the seams. Any dried white wax remaining can be melted using a hairdryer and worked in with the brush.

Animal magic

Crocodile teeth, although pretty terrifying to look at, are not made for chewing. Crocs have 24 teeth that they use to grasp and crush prey, then they swallow it whole! To aid digestion they also swallow small stones, which help grind up food in their stomachs.

Do you remember?

Going to work on an egg

Advice on eggs has see-sawed over the decades, but in the Fifties a whole advertising campaign hammered home that having an egg for breakfast was the best way to start the day. More than £12 million was spent on this campaign by the UK's Egg Marketing Board.

Recipe of the week

TUNA SALAD

Serves: 2 Prep: 5 mins Cook: 2 mins

75g (3oz) trimmed fine green beans, halved
400g (14oz) can cannellini beans, drained and rinsed
2 plum tomatoes, cut into chunks
6cm (2½in) piece cucumber, cut into chunks
50g (2oz) pitted black olives
2 tbsp French dressing
220g (8oz) tuna in spring water, drained
Handful parsley, chopped

1 Cook the green beans in boiling water for 3 mins, drain and cool. Mix in the cannellini beans, tomatoes, cucumber and olives.
2 Stir in the dressing, tuna and parsley, then season.
Waitrose

12 SUNDAY

13 MONDAY

14 TUESDAY

15 WEDNESDAY

16 THURSDAY

17 FRIDAY

18 SATURDAY

Blast from the past

MUD AND RED RUM

When I was five in 1977 I went to the Heathfield agricultural show which is held in Sussex every year in May. I went with my dad and my granddad who had a livestock business that transported farmers' cattle to the show. Once we'd arrived, the cowman and my dad unloaded the lorry and settled the cattle into their pens, then it was time to explore the show.

There was lots to see including country crafts, show jumping and dog shows. Red Rum was there with his jockey, Bob Champion. Red Rum bent his head down for me to give him a pat. I didn't know he was a famous race horse – he just seemed like a lovable giant to me.

I was wearing my new rainbow wellies and it was raining quite hard so there was lots of water to splash about in. I managed to get my wellies stuck in the mud so my dad had to pick me up and carry me. We had our dinner sitting on straw bales in the back of the lorry watching all the cars and vans getting stuck in the mud and having to be pulled out by tractors.
Sharon Smith, Merthyr Tydfil

Where did that come from?
'A baker's dozen'
This is believed to come from medieval times when English bakers selling a dozen loaves would throw in an extra one. They did this to make sure they weren't penalised for selling 'underweight' bread, a sin for which they could be fined, pilloried or even flogged meaning that 13th load could save them from sure punishment.

Old-fashioned household tips

Supermarket-cut flowers usually come with a packet of food to help the blooms last longer, but for homegrown flowers, keep them in an apple cider vinegar and sugar solution and if you have room, pop them in the fridge overnight.

Animal magic

Killer whales, pilot whales and humans are the only species that go through the menopause and continue to survive for many years without reproducing. All other animals produce offspring until they die.

Do you remember?

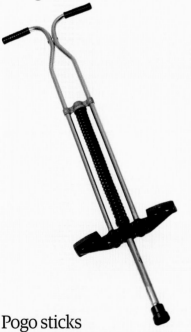

Pogo sticks
The culprit behind many a scraped knee and broken front teeth, the pogo stick was nevertheless the thing all Seventies children begged their parents for. Invented in 1919, in the Twenties the New York Hippodrome staged entire shows with chorus girls on pogo sticks.

Recipe of the week

ASPARAGUS CIGARS

Makes: 16 Prep: 15 mins Cook: 20 mins

2 bundles of asparagus
4 sheets of ready-made filo pastry
50g (2oz) butter, melted
2 handfuls of finely grated Parmesan
Salt and black pepper

1 Pre-heat the oven to 190°C/375°F/Gas Mark 5
2 Cook the asparagus for 3 mins in boiling water. Drain and cool, then dry thoroughly with a clean tea towel.
3 Take one sheet of filo pastry and brush lightly with butter. Cut each piece into four. Place each asparagus spear along the bottom of your filo piece and roll snugly.
4 Brush the outsides with butter again, then scatter with Parmesan and seasoning.
5 Bake on a lined tray for 15-18 mins until golden brown and crispy.
British asparagus

19 SUNDAY

20 MONDAY

21 TUESDAY

22 WEDNESDAY

23 THURSDAY

24 FRIDAY

25 SATURDAY

Blast from the past

A MIRROR IMAGE

One of the most memorable days of my life was May 21, 2014 when I attended the Queen's garden party at Buckingham Palace. My name had been put forward for an invitation due to my dedicated service to the NHS, having worked for a GP surgery for 32 years.

After much searching, I purchased my outfit which was a black dress with appliquéd blue flowers and a blue bolero. To complete the look, I had a matching feather fascinator. Other guests came from all over the world, some were dressed in their national costume and others in uniform.

After we had taken afternoon tea, I popped into the Ladies to powder my nose. They were very posh portaloos with large mirrors. As I came out and admired my reflection, I couldn't believe my eyes. Opposite me was a lady wearing the same dress and bolero, although she had a different hat. We looked at each other and had a good laugh. There were 8,000 people at the garden party and there we were, dressed like twins!

However, the amazing coincidence didn't spoil my special day at all.
Hazel Clarke, Wimborne

Where did that come from?
'Brass monkey weather'
We've all known the freezing, bitterly cold days that give rise to the 'brass monkeys' expression. The longer version of this phrase is 'cold enough to freeze the balls off a brass monkey' and comes from when brass triangles - nicknamed monkeys - would support stacks of iron cannon-balls on sailing ships which would freeze in cold weather, causing the balls to fall off.

Old-fashioned household tips

When it comes to DIY, removing tacks and nails with a claw hammer can, if you're not careful, scratch or dent surfaces. To give yourself a bit of protection, try sticking a small strip of foam across the top (or eye) of the hammer.

Animal magic

While the elephant has the longest gestation period of any land animal at around 22 months, scientists estimate the frilled shark tops this with a gestation period of a whopping 42 months! In comparison hamsters have one of the shortest, typically lasting just 16-23 days.

Do you remember?

Vim

First launched in 1904, the name Vim comes from the Latin word meaning 'vigour' or 'force' and certainly got to work on our grease and grime as a popular household staple. In the US it was the sponsor of the CBS show The Lucy Show starring Lucille Ball.

Recipe of the week

CHEESE AND APPLE CROQUETAS

Makes: 16 Prep: 20 mins Cook: 15 mins

2 large baking potatoes
60g (2½oz) Manchego cheese, grated
30g (1oz) Parmesan, grated
3 Pink Lady® apples (grated and drained)
2 pinches sea salt
10 tbsp plain flour
2 whisked eggs
100g (4oz) panko breadcrumbs

1 Cook the potatoes in a microwave or oven until cooked through. Scrape out the potato flesh and mash.
2 Combine the Manchego cheese, Parmesan, apples and salt to the potatoes and make 16 balls out of the mixture.
3 Roll the balls in the plain flour then dip them in the whisked eggs and then finish by rolling them in the breadcrumbs.
4 Heat a deep pan with enough oil to cover the croquetas. Add them to the hot oil and fry on a medium heat until golden brown. Drain on kitchen roll and serve immediately with a tasty dip.
Pink Lady

26 SUNDAY

27 MONDAY

28 TUESDAY

29 WEDNESDAY

30 THURSDAY

31 FRIDAY

1 SATURDAY

Blast from the past

HAPPY TIMES TOGETHER

I love this photo taken nearly 20 years ago because it reminds me of the lovely days when I was in my 70s. I am second from the left in the blue skirt and top. Unfortunately, my husband Robin is not in the picture as he is behind the camera. He was Welsh and his family had a lovely holiday home in North Wales.

We belonged to a close group of friends in our village and we used to take them there for a few nights every May. Robin would arrange to take the group to interesting places, some of which were not known to the public. Once we visited an old cottage that had a collection of chairs awarded to past Eisteddfod festival winners and another time we were shown around an underground dam that generated electricity. As he came from a big family, Robin would bump into someone he knew almost everywhere we went.

We had a picnic lunch every day and in the evenings dined at the local bistro. We really enjoyed being together and those of us of the group that are still here meet every week for coffee.

Roberta Price, Preston

Where did that come from?

'By the skin of one's teeth'

Meaning 'narrowly' or 'barely', this comes from the Book of Job in which Job is subjected to awful trials by Satan before he is finally relieved by God. Here he compared the narrow margin of his escape from Satan to the shallow skin or porcelain of a tooth which is barely more than a hair's breadth.

Old-fashioned household tips

Don't waste your food. To keep vegetables such as cucumbers fresher for longer, keep the end and when you've sliced off what you need, place the end back on and put a cocktail stick through it. This will help to keep it fresher for longer.

Animal magic

It's estimated that there are around one billion sheep worldwide, with more than 30 million in the UK. In Britain, an adult sheep produces one fleece a year and a proficient shearer can shear around 200 fleeces per day!

Do you remember?

Spam fritters

Whether you groaned or whooped when you spotted spam fritters on the menu for school dinners (again), they were a regular occurrence when we were at school. First introduced during rationing, their popularity continued well past then, commonly served with chips and mushy peas.

Recipe of the week

SPANISH POTATO, PRAWN & CHORIZO SALAD

Serves: 2 Prep: 20 mins Cook: 15 mins

100g (4oz) baby/new potatoes, halved
50g (2oz) chorizo sausage, thinly sliced
1 yellow pepper, de-seeded and sliced
8 cherry tomatoes, cut in half
2 garlic cloves, crushed
1 tbsp olive oil
150g (5oz) raw king prawns, shelled
Juice of ½ lemon
2 handfuls of spinach

1 Boil the potatoes for 6-7 mins, drain and set aside.
2 Fry the chorizo and yellow pepper over a medium heat until the oils from the chorizo come out and the peppers soften. Add the potatoes, tomatoes and garlic and continue cooking for about 5 mins. Tip into a mixing bowl.
3 Place the pan back onto the heat, add the olive oil and when hot, fry the prawns until they turn orange.
4 Serve with spinach and squeeze the lemon over.
Lakeland

2 SUNDAY

3 MONDAY

4 TUESDAY

5 WEDNESDAY

6 THURSDAY

7 FRIDAY

8 SATURDAY

Blast from the past

THE WONDER OF WOOLIES

As a teenager in the Sixties I loved to go shopping down the high street on Saturday morning. Woolworth's was the store my friends and I headed for as it stocked a wide selection of goods at reasonable prices. I could spend my wages of £5 5s on all manner of goodies.

The make-up counter, offering brands such as Rimmel and Miners, was a good starting point. I used to apply panstick foundation to my lips to give myself the 'pale and interesting' look. My favourite perfume was Evening in Paris, but you could also buy Californian Poppy and my mum's favourite, White Fire.

There was a record department selling Embassy records which were cover versions of the popular hits of the day. Sometimes we would go to the photo booth and have four photos taken of ourselves (they were the Sixties version of today's selfies). The flash always went off before we were ready for it and this would set us off into fits of giggles.

Our last purchase was from the sweet counter and the choice for me was always Melba fudge. A quarter of a pound in a paper bag would last until I reached the bus stop!

Helen Vanstone, Plymouth

Where did that come from?

'To be bankrupt'

You might think this means to literally break a bank but it actually comes from the 16th Century when moneylenders carried out their business on benches – 'banca' in Italian. When a money-dealer became insolvent, his work bench was broken and the phrase 'banca rotta' meaning 'broken bench' later morphed into the English word 'bankrupt', meaning someone who's gone out of business.

Old-fashioned household tips

If your new leather shoes are a little bit tight there's an easy to way to stretch them. Push a large potato, peeled and shaped, into the shoe and leave it in there overnight. As a bonus, it'll help remove any odour and if your shoes are faded, you can spruce them up a little by rubbing the potato over them.

Animal magic

The secret of eternal youth has been discovered by a jellyfish called the Turritopsis Dohrnii. Found in the Mediterranean Sea, instead of dying this jellyfish species renews itself into a younger version of itself! It shrinks in size and retracts its tentacles and then just starts its life-cycle again.

Do you remember?

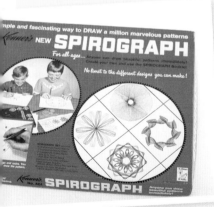

Spirographs

There was something completely hypnotising about this geometric drawing toy. While there'd always be that clever so-and-so at school who told us how it made mathematical roulette curves, technically known as hypotrochoids and epitrochoids, we just loved the pretty patterns we could create in moments.

Recipe of the week

BABY POTATO SALAD WITH HERBY CRÈME FRAÎCHE

Serves: 4 Prep: 15 mins Cook: 20 mins

500g (1lb 2oz) baby new potatoes, scrubbed
300g (10½ oz) green beans, trimmed
6 salad onions, finely chopped
25g (1oz) fresh flat-leaf parsley, finely chopped
25g (1oz) pack fresh mint, finely chopped
200ml (½pt) tub crème fraîche
2 tbsp fresh basil, leaves only
1 tbsp oil

1 Place the potatoes in a large pan of cold water and boil. Cook for 10 mins, adding the green beans for the last 5 mins until both are tender. Drain and then set aside to cool completely.
2 In a large bowl, mix the salad onions and chopped parsley and mint with the crème fraîche. Add the potatoes and beans and toss gently to combine.
3 Season to taste and serve topped with the basil and drizzled with oil.

Waitrose

9 SUNDAY

10 MONDAY

11 TUESDAY

12 WEDNESDAY

13 THURSDAY

14 FRIDAY

15 SATURDAY

Blast from the past

GLORIOUS DEVON

I treasure this photo of my great-grandfather taken with his horses around the turn of the last century. Although I never knew him, my family told me he was a very hardworking man - as they all were.

Born in Wales, I was adopted at the age of six weeks and had an idyllic childhood in Devon. My cousins lived in the same road so we always played together, games such as hopscotch. There was not much traffic to disturb us in the Fifties. At other times we used to go to the beach with my dog Kim who lived to the grand old age of 21. We lived near The Byes, a lovely riverside walk. In the spring we picked primroses, packed them with moss and sent them to our aunt in London. The post was very reliable so she always got them the next morning.

My dad grew all our fruit and vegetables and Mum cooked everything from scratch. She even made her own salad cream as well as a lovely Devonshire apple cake. Although none of us were well off financially we were rich with love and freedom and good country food.

Hazel Clapp, Sidmouth

Where did that come from?

'To be on a level pegging'

It's assumed this comes from the card game cribbage, with a bit of influence from darts. When darts was first played in pubs, players used the pegs of an old cribbage board to tot up the scores. As cribbage uses a 61 holed-board, when the scores were equal, the pegs in the board literally looked level.

Old-fashioned household tips

Put your ironing board up to use as a handy table when wrapping Christmas presents. Place your tape and labels where you'd normally have your iron and have it at perfect sitting or standing height with easy access to all sides of the gift.

Animal magic

Butterflies survive on an all-liquid diet, but did you know they can't live on sugary nectar alone? Some butterflies will even drink from muddy puddles to top up their mineral needs. You may also spot them finding watery nourishment from rotting fruit, dung and tree sap.

Do you remember?

A teasmade

If you got married in the Sixties or Seventies, chances are one of your wedding gifts was a teasmade. We never did quite get over the surprise of being able to have a cup of tea ready for us first thing in the morning.

Recipe of the week

BARBECUED PINEAPPLE WEDGES WITH CHOCOLATE AND COCONUT

Serves: 4 Prep: 10 mins Cook: 7 mins

25g (1oz) light soft brown sugar
½ tsp ground cinnamon
1 medium pineapple, cut into quarters, skinned and cored but with leaves left on
A little oil, for brushing
15g (½oz) dark chocolate shavings
15g (½oz) coconut flakes

1 In a bowl, mix the sugar and cinnamon, and sprinkle over all sides of the pineapple. Leave to sit for around 10 mins so the pineapple juice dissolves the sugar.
2 Place the pineapple wedges core side down on the barbecue, and cook for 3-5 mins or until golden brown. Carefully turn the wedges over so the core side is now facing up and grill for a further 3-5 mins.
3 Scatter the chocolate shavings on the top of each wedge, sprinkle over the coconut and grill for a further 1-2 mins, or until the coconut is lightly toasted and the chocolate has melted. Serve immediately.
Lakeland

16 SUNDAY

17 MONDAY

18 TUESDAY

19 WEDNESDAY

20 THURSDAY

21 FRIDAY

22 SATURDAY

Blast from the past

LONG HOT SUMMERS

Here I am with my sister Leesa and our cousin Alyson (I am the little girl in the middle). We appear to have had the photo taken outside my grandparents' caravan at Lodge Farm near Tenby in Pembrokeshire. I think this would have been around 1965.

I love our outfits, the expression on Alyson's face and the old camera that Leesa is holding – but I don't love my chubby legs! (I still have those, unfortunately.)

We used to spend a fortnight every summer in the caravan. In those days I used to get a bit fed up with going to the same place year after year, despite the wonderful beaches that we visited. It must have rained sometimes, but I only remember it being sunny and the sea sparkling. It used to be so hot sometimes that we'd burn our legs on the car seats after a day on the beach at Saundersfoot or Tenby.

I missed Pembrokeshire so much after our family holidays came to an end that I ended up moving here, although those long hot summers now seem to be a distant memory!
Judi James, Pembroke

Where did that come from?
'In a nutshell'
While this phrase for being concise has been used as a saying since Shakespeare's times, it actually harks back to an ancient story described by the Roman scholar Pliny in AD 77. He recounts when the great philosopher Cicero saw a copy of Homer's epic poem, the Iliad, written on a piece of parchment so small it could fit into the shell of a walnut.

Old-fashioned household tips

If you find some unwanted visitors in your house in summer, make your bug repellent by mixing equal parts Borax and sugar. It's great at keeping cockroaches, ants and other household pests at bay. Be sure to keep out of the way of pets and children.

Animal magic

The loveable Nemo made a name for this comical fish, but actually not all clownfish are orange. It's definitely a male-dominated species though, as all eggs hatch as males. Once mature they form a pair and the more dominant fish will then change to become a female!

Do you remember?

Bell-bottom trousers

They were a nightmare in a rain shower but the height of fashion in the Sixties and Seventies. Best worn with Cuban heels, clogs or Chelsea boots, they flared out from the calf and had curved hems. Sonny and Cher were particular fans.

Recipe of the week

HEALTHY FISH & CHIPS

Serves: 4 Prep: 20 mins Cook: 35 mins

75g (3oz) wholewheat couscous
Zest and juice 1 lemon
1½ tsp LoSalt
2 tbsp chopped chives
4 skinless, boneless cod or haddock fillets
1 medium egg, beaten
200g (7oz) vine on cherry tomatoes
750g (1lb 6oz) King Edward potatoes
1 tbsp oil
½ tsp paprika

1 Preheat the oven to 220ºC/425ºF/Gas Mark 7. Place the couscous in a small bowl. Heat the lemon juice for 30 secs in a microwave and make up to 100ml (4 fl oz) with boiling water and pour over the couscous with the zest, cover and leave for 5 mins. Fluff up with a fork and mix in ½ tsp salt and the chives.
2 Dip the fish in the egg and coat in the couscous, place on a large greased baking tray with the cherry tomatoes.
3 Cut the potatoes into chunky chips. Toss with oil, paprika and remaining 1 tsp salt and spread out on another large greased baking tray, bake in the top part of the oven for 10 mins. Add the fish tray below and cook for a further 20 mins, then remove and leave the chips to cook for a final 5 mins until golden. Serve the chips with the fish and tomatoes.
Losalt

23 SUNDAY

24 MONDAY

25 TUESDAY

26 WEDNESDAY

27 THURSDAY

28 FRIDAY

29 SATURDAY

Blast from the past

MY CANADIAN ADVENTURE

This photo was taken in June 1954 when I was ten. I had just arrived in Canada with my cousins, Joe and Jessica. (That's me on the right.) After sailing across the Atlantic, we had arrived in Quebec and been given gifts by relatives who had emigrated there the year before. Jessica and I had a doll each and Joe was given a cowboy outfit, complete with toy gun.

We stayed in Newmarket, Ontario, where we attended school and were taught by very strict teachers. The other children made fun of our English accents so we soon learned to adapt and fit in. When not attending school we had some wonderful family times, swimming in the lake in the summer months and visiting places of interest. We drove 2,000 miles to Missouri to visit our Aunt Jess who had emigrated there as a GI bride after the war.

In November 1955 it was time for me to return to my mother and family in England. Accompanied by my grandmother, I sailed back to Southampton on the Queen Elizabeth. After a short stay, my grandmother returned to her life in Canada.   **Jacqueline Pomeroy, Brighton**

Where did that come from?

'Mind your Ps and Qs'

Now used to remind people to say 'please' and 'thank you', this saying actually has nothing to do with politeness and everything to do with the printing press. Back in the early days of printing, a 'p' would sit next to a 'q' in the type case meaning it was ever so easy to accidentally make a typo, pressing one letter instead of the other.

Old-fashioned household tips

The secret to making perfectly baked biscuits is to try and keep the dough as cool as possible. Once you've cut out your biscuits with cutters pop them on a baking tray in the freezer for a few minutes. This will ensure they're all at the same temperature and will bake evenly.

Animal magic

An adult giraffe's tongue can be up to 50cm long, so long they can even lick their own ears! The tongue is coated in an antiseptic saliva, which is thought to help protect it from thorns when nibbling on acacia tree leaves.

Do you remember?

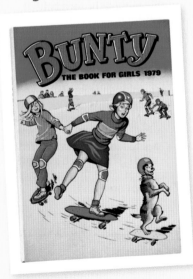

Bunty magazine

One of our favourite-ever comics, Bunty had everything we needed from stories to letters, competitions and puzzle pages. A highlight was the long-running story of The Four Marys in the weekly comic, as well as the release of the Christmas and summer Bunty annuals.

Recipe of the week

OPEN SALMON TART

Serves: 8 Prep: 30 mins Cook: 25 mins

400g (14oz) puff pastry
1 egg, beaten (for glazing)
300ml (10½fl oz) low-fat crème fraîche
3 tbsp low-fat mayonnaise
2 tbsp creamed horseradish
1 tbsp fresh lemon juice
250g (9oz) hot smoked salmon flakes

1 Heat the oven to 200°C/400°F/Gas Mark 6. Roll out the pastry on a lightly floured surface and cut out eight 10cm (4in) squares. With a knife, mark a square 1cm (½in) in from the edge all the way around (without cutting right through the pastry) on each. Brush with egg and bake for 20-25 mins.
2 Meanwhile, beat together the crème fraîche, mayonnaise, horseradish and lemon juice. Chill until required.
3 Remove the cooked squares from the oven. Lift off the top few layers of the inner squares of pastry and discard. Return the cases to the oven for 2 mins, then cool.
4 Spoon some crème fraîche mixture into the hollow of each tart, top with hot smoked salmon flakes and garnish with fresh dill, lemon zest and cracked black pepper.

Morrisons

30 SUNDAY

1 MONDAY

2 TUESDAY

3 WEDNESDAY

4 THURSDAY

5 FRIDAY

6 SATURDAY

Blast from the past

A FISHY STORY

This is my husband, Mike, and me on holiday in New England. Our reason for being in that part of America was a result of my researches into my family history during which I discovered a long-lost cousin, Eliza, who lived in Cape Cod. We met her in London when she came over to the UK and she invited us to visit her in New England.

Three years ago we managed to make the trip. We stayed in a wonderful house in Provincetown which can be seen behind us in the photo. The boat belonged to our hostess who went out fishing regularly so we dined on lobster and mussels fresh from the sea. Eliza had a restaurant called The Wicked Oyster so we had a delicious meal there too.

One of the many highlights of our stay was a whale-watching trip when we spotted several varieties of whales. The trip was made even more special when a pod of dolphins escorted us back to Provincetown. We felt very privileged to have stayed in such a unique place and will never forget the experience.
Pat Gannon-Leary, Gateshead

Where did that come from?

'Go doolally'

It's a funny word but doolally is actually an Anglicisation of a real place in India. Deolali was where soldiers from the British army would wait, often for months, to be taken back to Britain after their duty in India. There was nothing to do here and many went mad with boredom, giving rise to the phrase that means to lose your mind today.

Old-fashioned household tips

If you have laminate or wooden flooring you'll want to avoid scratching it when moving a large piece of furniture or white goods. If whatever you're moving doesn't have wheels, simply place an egg box underneath each of the legs.

Animal magic

Only male peacocks are actually called peacocks, females are called peahens and offspring are called peachicks. All peachicks look identical to their mothers at birth. The males begin to change colour at around six months old, but don't grow their magnificent tail feathers until they're three years old.

Do you remember?

Spinning tops
We could while away literally hours mastering the exact twist of the fingers that would see our spinning tops go for far longer than our friends'. Based on an idea that goes back to antiquity it's amazing such a simple toy used to provide so much amusement.

Recipe of the week

STRAWBERRY AND RHUBARB ICE-POPS

Serves: 6 Prep: 5 mins Freeze: 3 hours

200g (7oz) strawberries (cut into quarters)
300g (10½oz) Alpro Strawberry with Rhubarb or strawberry yogurt

1 Purée 150g (5oz) of the quartered strawberries using a handblender.
2 Add the remaining strawberries to the strawberry purée and mix together.
3 Pour the strawberry mixture into 6 ice-lolly moulds and top up with the Alpro.
4 Leave for at least 3 hours until lollies are frozen.
Alpro

7 SUNDAY

8 MONDAY

9 TUESDAY

10 WEDNESDAY

11 THURSDAY

12 FRIDAY

13 SATURDAY

Blast from the past

MY FIRST GARDEN

This watering-can moment marks a watershed in my young life. The photo was taken in 1948 when I was six years old. I had just moved with my parents and baby brother to a Victorian terraced house that they had bought.

My father, a keen gardener, was thrilled to have a garden of his own for the first time – albeit a very small one. It was around this time that he made a window box out of scraps of wood. He painted it sky blue and my mother embellished it by painting a picture of rabbits. Having filled the box with soil, my father planted it with lobelias. This was to be my 'garden'. I was enthralled by the deep, rich blue of the lobelias and it was the beginning of a lifelong passion for gardening. It wasn't long before I was helping my father on his allotment.

Now my husband and I have our own Victorian house with a small garden and we also have an allotment. Two years ago, our garden won a local award. I hope to inspire other people the way my father inspired me nearly 70 years ago. A windowbox is a good starting point!

Mary Cook, Gainsborough

Where did that come from?

'Skeleton in the closet'

Until the 1830s it was illegal to dissect human bodies, which caused issues for the medical schools and doctors curious about exploring human anatomy for their research. So grave-robbers and murderers would provide these medical professionals with the bodies they required which had to be hidden in cupboards in case of raids, meaning many people literally had skeletons in their closets.

Old-fashioned household tips

Slugs can be a gardener's nightmare, munching their way through your healthy plants, but if you're a coffee drinker, don't throw away those coffee grounds. As well as a soil additive that's good for leafy plants such as tomatoes, roses and rhododendrons, it's also great at deterring hungry slugs.

Animal magic

We all know that ants for their size are super strong, but did you know that there are an estimated one million ants for every human! They also live longer than all other insects, with some species living up to 30 years.

Do you remember?

The Tufty Club

Tufty Fluffytail was born in 1953, and used by the Royal Society for the Prevention of Accidents to teach simple safety messages to children. Tufty was joined in his adventures by the likes of Minnie Mole and the naughty Willy Weasel.

Recipe of the week

BAKED SPINACH & MUSHROOM FRITTATA

Serves: 4 Prep: 15 mins Cook: 30 mins

1 tsp olive oil
3 garlic cloves
1 small leek
400g (14oz) button mushrooms, sliced thickly
200g (7oz) baby spinach leaves
2 eggs
6 egg whites
125ml (4 fl oz) skimmed milk
40g (1½oz) cheddar, coarsely grated
1 tomato, sliced

1 Preheat the oven to 150°C/300°F/Gas Mark 2
2 Grease a deep 23cm (9in) round cake tin and line the base with baking parchment.
3 Fry the garlic, leek and mushrooms in a little oil, stirring occasionally, until the mushrooms are just tender. Add the spinach; cook until just wilted, then discard any liquid from the pan.
4 Whisk together the eggs, egg whites, milk and cheese, then stir in the vegetable mixture.
5 Pour the mixture into the prepared tin and top with the tomato. Bake for about 25 mins or until just set, then place under a hot grill to brown.
Lakeland

14 SUNDAY

15 MONDAY

16 TUESDAY

17 WEDNESDAY

18 THURSDAY

19 FRIDAY

20 SATURDAY

Blast from the past

A DAY OUT IN BLACKPOOL

Here I am with two old pals from the Fifties. We worked together in a factory called Rists Wires and Cables. We had lots of fun and laughter together and we were told off many times for misbehaving and time-wasting, but we never changed.

This photo was taken when the three of us went on a trip to Blackpool with my eldest son, Paul (who is now in his 60s!). We enjoyed a paddle in the sea, ice-cream cones, playing the penny slot machines and even had a ride on the donkeys. I didn't enjoy that very much as my donkey was bigger than the others and started to gallop. I was scared of falling off, but all my friends did was burst their sides laughing at me.

We all had a good sleep on our return journey home on the bus. We were shattered after running round the beach all day after young Paul.

My two pals are no longer here, but they are certainly not forgotten. They were happy days and it's good to remember them.

Mrs B Jones, Newcastle under Lyme

Where did that come from?

'To butter someone up'

Sounds messy, but this saying for flattering someone to make them more pliable to your requests, comes from an ancient Indian custom that involved throwing ghee butter at statues of the gods when they wanted to ask for favours. This was thought to be an act of humility and people did this in the hopes that the gods would look favourably upon them.

Old-fashioned household tips

While perfectly fine to eat, brown ageing bananas can be off-putting and as they ripen can attract fruit flies. Stop your bananas going brown by covering the end of the bunch or individual bananas tightly in duct or packing tape, pushing out any air bubbles as you go.

Animal magic

The largest creature on earth, the blue whale can grow up to a whopping 33 metres in length and can live to between 80-90 years old. Calves are born around 7m in length and can drink more than 500 litres of their mother's milk a day!

Do you remember?

Aqua Manda perfume

With its brown, orange and green retro pattern, Aqua Manda perfume perfectly captured the spirit of the swinging Sixties and Seventies. Often advertised on Radio Luxembourg, it was generally stocked in Boots and other department stores and has a sweet orange blossom scent.

Recipe of the week

TACO SALAD

Serves: 4 Prep: 15 mins

2 little gem lettuces, sliced
400g (14oz) can red kidney beans, drained and rinsed
50g (2oz) pitted black olives, sliced
100g (4oz) radishes, sliced
2 sticks celery, sliced
2 ripe avocados
150ml (5fl oz) carton soured cream
2 tbsp pibil paste (or other chilli paste)
Juice of 1 lime
1 pack of taco shells
Handful of coriander, chopped

1 Mix together the little gems, kidney beans, olives, radishes, celery and 1 diced avocado in a large bowl.
2 Place the remaining avocado, soured cream, pibil paste and lime juice in a small food processor and blitz until smooth, then season. Toss half of this into the salad.
3 Spoon the salad into the taco shells and drizzle the remaining dressing on top. Sprinkle over the coriander and serve.
Lakeland

21 SUNDAY

22 MONDAY

23 TUESDAY

24 WEDNESDAY

25 THURSDAY

26 FRIDAY

27 SATURDAY

Blast from the past

TRAVELLING SOLO

Having owned a hotel and then a restaurant with my husband before he died five years ago, I had always fancied doing a foreign cookery course. Two years ago, I plucked up the courage to go on my first solo holiday doing Italian cookery, wine tasting and sightseeing.

My nervousness soon abated when I was able to pick out my fellow travellers at the airport. Some of them were seasoned solo travellers and others were first-timers like myself. We soon grouped together and bonded even further after our introductory drinks reception at the hotel. The next day we launched into our first Italian cookery experience (the photo shows me making pasta!), followed by a wonderful three-course lunch supplied by the owners of the Tuscan olive farm.

We visited vineyards, had another cookery lesson at a castle and were taken on sightseeing expeditions with Italian lessons given on the way by our excellent courier. I had the time of my life, making friends who were in the same boat as myself. I now have the confidence to go somewhere on my own if I can't find a friend to accompany me.

Diana Drayton, Netley Abbey

Where did that come from?

'Cat got your tongue'

There's two possible origins to this saying and both are pretty unpleasant. The first is from the English navy which had a type of whip called the 'cat o'nine tails', used for flogging and thought to cause so much pain it would leave victims speechless. The other idea is that it's from the practice of cutting out the tongues of liars and feeding them to cats.

Old-fashioned household tips

If your shower head has gone from Niagara Falls to a dribble, it's more than likely clogged by limescale. After your shower, fill a sandwich bag with baking soda and vinegar and tie it around the showerhead using an elastic band. Leave this to soak overnight and any debris should come off easily with an old toothbrush.

Animal magic

Girl power started way before the Spice Girls it seems! The whiptail lizard is an all-female species that doesn't need males to reproduce. They produce asexually, but still deliver a full chromosome count, so offspring don't suffer any genetic weaknesses.

Do you remember?

The beehive hair-do

Dusty Springfield had one as did all The Ronettes and before long we were all begging our hairdressers to tease our hair into a beehive. It required so much back-coming and hairspray, it really is a wonder our hair ever survived.

Recipe of the week

PEARL BARLEY, BEETROOT AND BROCCOLI SALAD

Serves: 2 Prep: 10 mins Cook: 20 mins

1 large beetroot, peeled, cut into wedges
1 medium onion, cut into wedges
2 tsp olive oil
200g (7oz) broccoli florets
100g (4oz) pearl barley
1 tbsp tahini
1 tbsp warm water
1 tbsp lemon juice
6 tbsp fresh flat-leaf parsley leaves

1 Preheat oven to 220°C/425°F/Gas Mark 7.
2 Place the beetroot and onion on a large oven tray, drizzle with oil. Roast for about 20 mins. Add broccoli and roast for a further 15 mins or until golden and tender.
3 Boil the pearl barley in salted water for 40 mins or until tender. Drain well.
4 Mix together the tahini, warm water and lemon juice.
5 Toss the roasted vegetables and parsley through the warm pearl barley. Drizzle with the tahini dressing and serve.
Lakeland

28 SUNDAY

29 MONDAY

30 TUESDAY

31 WEDNESDAY

1 THURSDAY

2 FRIDAY

3 SATURDAY

Blast from the past

EMERGENCY BRIDESMAID

My wedding day was memorable for a series of near disasters, beginning with my chief bridesmaid arriving on the doorstep to announce that her mother had been rushed to hospital. I said: "Don't worry, we'll sort something out – you must be with her."

The other bridesmaid, my 14-year-old sister Dorothy, was not happy about being on her own so we asked her friend Carole if she would stand in at the last minute. Carole was thrilled to be asked, but the dress was too big for her. Instead of having time to get myself ready, I spent the morning tacking up the seams to make it a slimmer fit.

Meanwhile, another visitor arrived to announce that the little flower girl had measles and could not attend. After all that practice of scattering paper rose petals!

That was not the end of it. My mother realised that the bride's bouquet and the buttonholes had not arrived. No phones in 1955 so someone was sent to the florist, only to find that the flowers had been delivered to the groom's address.

As you can see from the photo of Carole and Dorothy, the wedding finally went ahead with no further hitches.

Edna Thomason, Stoke-on-Trent

Where did that come from?

'On the wagon'

Meaning to abstain from alcohol, this unsurprisingly comes from Prohibition times when alcohol was banned in the USA. At this time it was common to see water wagons going round cleaning the streets and people who swore to not drink alcohol would often joke that they would rather drink from the dirty water of the water wagon than drink alcohol.

Old-fashioned household tips

Venetian blinds can be time consuming to clean, but using an old odd clean sock can reduce the time taken on this tedious task. Wear it on your hand as you would a hand puppet and you can wipe each blind slat individually in seconds.

Animal magic

When flying, honey bees flap their wings around 200 times a second and can reach speeds of up to 20mph. Being fast is important to this species as to make just one pound of honey they need to visit around two million flowers and they're responsible for pollinating a third of the crops we eat.

Do you remember?

Viewmaster

Our young minds were well and truly blown by the Viewmaster stereoscope which conjured up amazing images before our very eyes. First introduced in 1939, early reels showed tourist attractions and views of travel hotspots and later cartoons and children's TV series.

Recipe of the week

MIXED BERRY GINGER ICE CREAM

Serves: 4 Prep: 5 mins

300g (10½oz) mixed frozen berries
300g (10½oz) Alpro Vanilla (or vanilla yogurt)
70g (3oz) stem ginger
1 tbsp of agave syrup

1 Add the frozen berries, Alpro or yogurt, stem ginger and agave syrup to a blender. Blend until smooth.
2 Scoop into bowls and serve immediately.
Alpro

4 SUNDAY

5 MONDAY

6 TUESDAY

7 WEDNESDAY

8 THURSDAY

9 FRIDAY

10 SATURDAY

Blast from the past

HAPPY CAMPERS

In the Fifties and Sixties my family spent many summer holidays at Trusville holiday camp near Mablethorpe on the bracing east coast of Lincolnshire. Of course, it was usually sunny in my memories although I recall us taking refuge in a bus shelter more than once on our way back from the town. The rain came in sideways!

As usual at this time in my life, whenever the camera came out I seemed to be missing a tooth. I was about seven when this photo was taken at one of the camp's fancy dress competitions for which I had improvised a costume. I wore my favourite dress which had Oriental ladies on it so I took two cups from our chalet and entered as 'Tea for Two'. I didn't win, but my dad stormed to victory in the knobbly knees competition so we went home happy.

They were proper beach holidays – I remember paddling in my ruched bathing costume, building sandcastles, donkey rides, catching crabs in a bucket and picnic lunches with ham and sand sandwiches. Happy days!

I believe Trusville park is still there, but I'm sure it has changed with the times and would be very different now.

Joy Harris, Peterborough

Where did that come from?

'To be caught red-handed'

This comes from a law that decreed if you butchered an animal that didn't belong to you, you had to be caught with the animal's blood on your hands to be prosecuted – having possession of the meat wasn't sufficient proof of guilt. Back then, being caught red-handed meant a death sentence, but now it tends to describe someone being caught in the middle of wrong-doing.

Old-fashioned household tips

To stop lingering odours from your kitchen bin, line it with a few sheets of clean newspaper and a sprinkling of bicarbonate of soda (baking soda) before putting your liner in. Each time you replace your liner, check the newspaper, if it's damp, simply remove, throw away and replace.

Animal magic

Aside from humans and chimpanzees, horses have one of the most expressive faces in the animal kingdom. Our equine friends can make 17 separate facial expressions and although that's ten fewer than us, it's one more than man's best friend.

Do you remember?

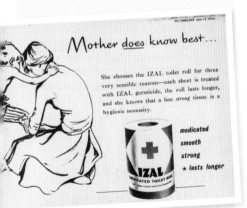

Mother does know best...

She chooses the IZAL toilet roll for three very sensible reasons—each sheet is treated with IZAL germicide, the roll lasts longer, and she knows that a fine strong tissue is a hygienic necessity.

medicated
smooth
strong
★ lasts longer

IZAL
MEDICATED TOILET ROLL

Izal loo roll
It might have looked more like tracing paper than toilet tissue, but Izal was something of a national institution, installed in school lavs and public conveniences the country over. It could be a bit scratchy and always had something of a disinfectant whiff.

Recipe of the week

STUFFED PICNIC LOAF

Serves: 8 Prep: 30 mins Cook: None

1 large round crusty loaf
Extra-virgin olive oil, to brush
300g (10½oz) cheddar cheese, sliced
8 sausages, cooked, cooled and sliced
3 medium vine-ripened tomatoes, sliced
75g (3oz) rocket
6 tbsp tomato chutney
Salt & pepper

1 Slice off the top of the loaf and set aside. Remove all the soft bread from inside, leaving the crust to form a case. Brush inside the loaf with a little olive oil.
2 Layer the cheese, sausage, tomato, rocket and chutney, seasoning as you go.
3 When the bread case is full, brush inside the bread lid with olive oil, pop back on and press to seal. Wrap tightly with a double layer of clingfilm, place in the fridge and weigh the lid down (we put a plate and tin of food on top). Refrigerate overnight.
4 To serve, unwrap and cut into wedges.
Lakeland

11 SUNDAY

12 MONDAY

13 TUESDAY

14 WEDNESDAY

15 THURSDAY

16 FRIDAY

17 SATURDAY

Blast from the past

TIMES WERE DIFFERENT

During the war when I was evacuated to Bedfordshire, my mother wrote to tell me that a new family had moved in two doors away and the little girl, Margaret, would like to meet me when I came home. We soon became friends and went to the same high school. When we were older we both worked in London for the Bank of England and both met our future husbands at around the same time.

We got engaged within a few months of each other and decided we'd like to go on holiday with our fiancés to the Isle of Wight. It wasn't as easy as it sounds because in those days permission was needed from both sets of parents. But permission was given and we set off by train and boat. When we arrived at our guesthouse in Ventnor we were told sternly: "You two girls will be sleeping here and the two boys will be over the road, but they can come here for their meals." How different from the way teenagers would be treated today!

This photo is of Margaret and me paddling on the beach at Ventnor. Margaret is the tall one.
Kathleen Marks, Kent

Where did that come from?

'Don't throw the baby out with the bathwater'

During the 1500s, most people bathed not much more than once a year and even then you'd share bathwater with your whole family. Men bathed first, followed by women, then children, meaning by the time a baby got in, the bath would be thick and cloudy and Mum had to be careful not to empty her baby out with the tub of water.

Old-fashioned household tips

Do you find it difficult to thoroughly clean a thin-necked glass bottle? A tried and tested way to clean the inside of a bottle is to pour a little bit of sand and water into the bottle. Shake thoroughly so the sand can agitate the dirt, allowing you to wash it away.

Animal magic

Research suggests dolphins are smarter than chimpanzees and as equally intelligent as humans. Scientists believe dolphins even give themselves names and have individual whistles to communicate with other pod members.

Do you remember?

Fine Fare

There was nothing quite like bagging a bargain midweek dinner from Fine Fare's Yellow Pack range. Having started as a single shop in 1951, Fine Fare was all over the country by the Seventies, stocking all the weekly essentials in one convenient place.

Recipe of the week

WARM POTATO & TUNA SALAD

Serves: 2 Prep: 10 mins Cook: 20 mins

350g (12oz) salad/baby potatoes, sliced in half
150g (5oz) runner beans, sliced into 2cm pieces
100g (4oz) curly kale, roughly chopped
1 small red onion, finely sliced
2 tbsp olive oil
Juice of 1 lemon
2 tins of tuna in spring water, drained
50g (2oz) sundried tomatoes, roughly chopped
50g (2oz) black pitted olives
20g (¾oz) sunflower seeds

1 Boil the potatoes in salted water until tender, drain and set aside. Once cooled, cut the potatoes into bite-size pieces.
2 Cook the beans in salted water for 4-5mins then add the kale and blanch for a few seconds then drain.
3 In a large serving bowl add the potatoes, runner beans, kale and red onion. Drizzle in the olive oil and lemon juice and mix well.
4 Add the tuna, sundried tomatoes and black olives, lightly mix and serve with a scattering of sunflower seeds.
lovepotatoes.co.uk

18 SUNDAY

19 MONDAY

20 TUESDAY

21 WEDNESDAY

22 THURSDAY

23 FRIDAY

24 SATURDAY

Blast from the past

A KNITTING YARN

Back in the Eighties, I fell in love with this pattern for a beautiful cardigan. Nylon carpet wool was very popular at the time and it was very reasonably priced, probably because it was sold in hanks that had to be wound into individual balls. I bought loads of it. It came in every colour imaginable and had a lovely sheen to it so I thought it would be ideal for this project.

It did take quite a while to knit, but it was well worth it as it fitted perfectly. I just loved it. So much so that I decided to wear it to attend the works' summer do on the following night. I could team it with some rust-colour trousers. Perfect.

A quick rinse to freshen it up was in order as it had been on the knitting needles so long. Being nylon, it would soon dry overnight. Mistake! No sooner had I placed it in the basin of warm soapy water than the colours ran. My beautiful cardi turned into a mucky, mud-coloured mess. It was soul destroying and quite some time before I wanted to knit anything again. But I kept the pattern and more than 30 years later, have just started to knit it once more.
Anne Orr via email

Where did that come from?
'Give the cold shoulder'
Now the ultimate sign of a frosty welcome, this phrase comes from medieval England when a host would give a subtle sign it was time for his or her guest to leave by offering a piece of cold meat from the shoulder of mutton, beef or pork. They usually got the message and slung their hook.

Old-fashioned household tips

It's a well-known fact that after time a salt shaker left in the kitchen will become clogged. This is because salt is naturally absorbent and will attract moisture in the air created by cooking. To help keep the salt free-flowing simply add a few grains of white rice to your shaker.

Animal magic

It isn't true that owls can rotate their heads a full 360 degrees, although they can rotate as far as 130 degrees in each direction. Owl eyes are fixed into their skulls and they can't turn them, so this head movement is essential for survival.

Do you remember?

Lifebuoy soap

Created by the Lever Brother soap factory in 1894, Lifebuoy was the first soap to use carbolic acid. This gave it that distinctive red colour and trademark medicinal smell. Originally only used by medical professionals, it later became a household essential.

Recipe of the week

SPANISH TORTILLAS

Serves: 12 Prep: 15 mins Cook: 18 mins

2 tbsp olive oil
2 medium potatoes, peeled, quartered and thinly sliced
1 small onion, thinly sliced
6 eggs
1 tbsp chopped fresh flat-leaf parsley
Salt and pepper

1 Preheat the oven to 200°C/400°F/Gas Mark 6.
2 Heat 1 tbsp olive oil in a large frying pan then cook the potatoes and onion over a medium heat for 20-25 mins until the potatoes are tender. Leave to cool for 10 mins.
3 Beat the eggs in a large bowl, add the parsley, cooked potatoes and onion, then mix and season well.
4 Lightly grease a bun tin with the remaining oil. Divide the mixture evenly into the holes, filling each three-quarters full.
5 Cook for 15-18 mins until golden. Leave to cool before removing the tortillas from the tin.
Lakeland

25 SUNDAY

26 MONDAY

27 TUESDAY

28 WEDNESDAY

29 THURSDAY

30 FRIDAY

31 SATURDAY

Blast from the past

MY NOT-SO-SHY MUM!

This photo of my mother standing outside our house brings back a vivid memory of the street party we had to celebrate VE Day at the end of the war. The ten families who lived in our row of houses organised a good evening, with a plate of food each, squash for the children and something more alcoholic for the grown-ups.

Then two tables were pushed together to make a stage. Several of the neighbours climbed up to entertain us with a song, a dance or a few jokes. In the midst of all this merriment my mother, who was the shyest, most private person ever, climbed up on to the 'stage' and recited: 'Little fly upon the wall, ain't you got no clothes at all? Ain't you got no blouse or skirt? Ain't you got a little shirt? Lumme, ain't you cold?'.

Everyone roared with laughter and clapped madly as my mother stood there smiling shyly and going very pink in the face. For the rest of the evening, I saw her talking and laughing with people. I was amazed. She was like a butterfly that had emerged from its chrysalis!
Pat Rose, Sidmouth

Where did that come from?

'To get out on the wrong side of the bed'

We've all done it but this saying for waking up in a bad mood comes from an old Roman superstition that said it was unlucky to get out of bed with your left leg first. In fact the left side was thought to be unlucky in general and some Romans, supposedly including Augustus Caesar, even believed it bad luck to put your left shoe on first.

Old-fashioned household tips

You only really need two sets of bedding per bed - one on the bed, one in the wash. The set will generally go in the wash and come out together, so when dry keep them organised by folding your duvet cover, sheets and any extra pillow cases and storing them inside your matching pillow case.

Animal magic

A group of parrots is called a pandemonium, a group of flamingos is called a flamboyance and a group of porcupines is called a prickle. Other surprising group names include a group of alligators being called a congregation, a group of giraffes is a tower and a group of hippos is called a crash!

Do you remember?

ONLY NEW CREAMY Prom
PASSES THE 'COMB-THROUGH' TEST

It's now Creamy Prom – the enriched flowing-cream home perm

Smooth it on—roll it up and rinse—
you've got yourself a Prom

Home perms

We'd go to great lengths in pursuit of beauty as youngsters, including letting our not particularly responsible friends and sisters loose with a bottle of perming lotion on our hair. If we were lucky, we sometimes got away without a completely singed scalp.

Recipe of the week

ROASTED TOMATO, CHICKPEA & HALLOUMI SALAD

Serves: 4 Prep: 5 mins Cook: 25 mins

Half a small red onion, chopped
1 tbsp red wine vinegar
2 tbsp olive oil
1 large courgette, halved lengthways, thickly sliced
400g (14oz) small tomatoes, halved
250g (9oz) halloumi cheese, sliced
Chilli oil or olive oil to drizzle
400g (14oz) tin chickpeas, rinsed

1 Preheat the oven to 220°C/425°F/Gas Mark 7. Toss the onion in the vinegar and 2 tbsp olive oil and set aside.
2 Put the courgettes and the tomatoes (cut side up) on a baking tray, season well and roast for 25 mins.
3. Preheat the grill. Drizzle the halloumi with a little chilli oil and grill until golden brown on each side.
4 Gently toss the chickpeas, parsley, roasted tomatoes and courgettes with the onion mixture.
5 Divide between plates and top with the halloumi. Serve with a green salad and crusty bread.
Lakeland

1 SUNDAY

2 MONDAY

3 TUESDAY

4 WEDNESDAY

5 THURSDAY

6 FRIDAY

7 SATURDAY

Blast from the past

COAST TO COAST BY BIKE

It's amazing what you can do if you try. I used to dream of doing the coast to coast cycle ride from Whitehaven to Tynemouth (140 miles), but thought I'd never actually get round to it. Then in August 1997 I decided to stop dreaming and start pedalling. I started off thinking 'I'll never be able to complete the ride' but although it was tough at times, it gave me a real buzz being so high up on the moors.

When I arrived in Tynemouth, it proved to be a memorable day in more ways than one. As I got my stamp of proof that I'd completed the ride, I looked down and saw from the headlines in a newspaper that Princess Diana had died. I felt so happy and yet so sad.

In the photo I am holding the trophy that my husband and children had engraved for me. Completing the ride gave me the confidence to do other things. I would love to do the ride from John O'Groats to Land's End one day. Who knows? You are never too old to try something new.

Margaret Dinsdale, Tyne and Wear

Where did that come from?

'To draw a blank'

When we forget something so absolutely we can't bring anything to mind, the saying we used to describe it reaches back to Elizabeth I who held national lotteries to recoup money for the throne. Lottery contestants wrote their name onto tickets and if you won, the back of your ticket had a prize written on it. If not, your ticket was blank.

Old-fashioned household tips

If you're going on holiday overseas, don't waste valuable baggage weight on travel irons. Minimise creasing by folding each garment in a dry cleaning bag or similar. When you get to your destination, remove from the bag and hang in the bathroom where the steam from your bath will naturally reduce the wrinkles in your clothing.

Animal magic

As if Jaws wasn't scary enough, did you know that shark's teeth grow continuously? They have multiple rows of teeth and when one falls out, another will push forward into the gap left behind. Some scientists believe that in a lifetime, a shark can produce up to 30,000 teeth.

Do you remember?

BIBA

It was the shop unlike anything we'd ever seen before when Barbara Hulanicki opened the doors to her pioneering fashion house Biba in 1964. With art deco inspired items and dreamy outfits, Barbara was even responsible for getting the mini-skirt on the high street.

Recipe of the week

ELDERFLOWER, STRAWBERRY AND ROSE SORBET

Serves: 6 Prep: 30 mins Cook: 15 mins

150g (5oz) white caster sugar
500g (1lb 2oz) fresh strawberries, wiped and hulled
125ml (4½floz) Belvoir Elderflower and Rose cordial
Juice of 1 lemon or lime

1 Gently heat the sugar in a pan with 250ml of water and allow to cool once dissolved.
2 Purée the strawberries in a food processor, add the cordial and lemon juice and blitz until well combined.
3 Add the cooled syrup to the strawberry mixture, mix well and chill in the fridge for several hours.
4 Spoon the sorbet into a covered container and freeze; take it out of the freezer every hour and beat it vigorously. After 4 hours it should be frozen and ready to enjoy.

Recipe by Karen Burns-Booth

8 SUNDAY

9 MONDAY

10 TUESDAY

11 WEDNESDAY

12 THURSDAY

13 FRIDAY

14 SATURDAY

Blast from the past

CARVED WITH PRIDE

When we were young we always went on holiday to Great Yarmouth or Skegness as we didn't have a car and they were the easiest places to get to by train or coach. Holidays were a big family affair that included various aunts and uncles so we all travelled together. The journey was almost as much fun as the holiday.

In 1953, we had planned to go to Sea Palling in Norfolk, but this was the summer after the floods that had devastated much of the North Sea coast and the caravan we'd booked had been washed away. Instead we stayed in a house with an old couple. It was a slightly odd arrangement as Mum had to buy our food and the lady of the house cooked it for us.

Her husband was a stonemason who made headstones and ornaments for graves. He had a big workshop at the bottom of the garden and after we'd had our tea I would go out and watch him at work. After a few days he let me have a go and I carved a small bird which I was really proud of. The photo shows my sister Pat and me, holding the bird.

Margaret Wiltshire, Leicester

Where did that come from?

'Blood is thicker than water'

The reason this saying doesn't always make sense is because we're not quoting the full saying which in the Bible reads as 'the blood of the covenant is thicker than the water of the womb'. This means bloodshed in battle bonds soldiers more strongly than simple genetics although we now wrongly typically use this to talk about the importance of family over everything else.

Old-fashioned household tips

If you have cans of deodorant, shaving foam or air freshener in your bathroom, you'll probably find they are prone to leaving rust rings on your surfaces. Paint the underside rim of the can with some clear nail varnish and let it dry upside down before using – this will help protect your tops and tiles.

Animal magic

Flamingos deliberately feed with their bills upside down and have a clever filtering system. In shallow water they use their feet to stir up food on the water bed. They then use their specially adapted bills to separate mud and silt from food using hairy structures in their bills called lamellae.

Do you remember?

FAB ice lollies

While the boys had Zooms, girls tucked into a FAB on a sunny day. Inspired by the Thunderbirds catchphrase F-A-B, the wrapping featured Lady Penelope and contained a strawberry and vanilla ice with the top dipped in chocolate and hundreds and thousands.

Recipe of the week

STUFFED LAMB BURGERS

Serves: 4 Prep: 10 mins Cook: 16 mins

500g (1lb 2oz) minced lamb
Salt and pepper
60g (2½oz) feta, crumbled
Small handful mint leaves, roughly chopped

1 Season the lamb well then divide into 8 portions and shape into patties.
2 Make a small well in each patty (you can do this by hand or with a burger press). Place a little of the feta and mint into the well, top with another patty and seal together. Refrigerate for 30 mins or until required.
3 Cook the burgers for 8 mins on each side or until cooked through.
Lakeland

15 SUNDAY

16 MONDAY

17 TUESDAY

18 WEDNESDAY

19 THURSDAY

20 FRIDAY

21 SATURDAY

Blast from the past

SUPERSTAR KNITTER

When Tom and I announced that we were going to get married on September 10, 1960, Mum said: "There's a knitting pattern I've been saving because I thought it would make a lovely wedding dress." Between March and September, she hand knitted my dress, six bridesmaids' dresses and her own lilac and white suit.

The nylon wool for my dress cost £6 and the small silver beads came in a packet of one thousand for ten shillings. In those days the wool came in skeins and had to be wound into balls. We stumbled across a problem when we had to thread the beads onto a strand of wool because a needle with an eye to take the wool was too large for the beads. Dad came to the rescue by fashioning a needle using five-amp fuse wire.

While Mum was knitting she made a diamond pattern with four beads in the centre. There were two panels in this diamond shape, one in the front and one in the back of the dress. The sides of the dress were knitted in stocking stitch.

I still have the dress and wore it on our 50th wedding anniversary.
Yvonne Parsons, Exmouth

Where did that come from?

'To let your hair down'
Anyone who's ever worn a fancy, tight hairdo knows the joy at letting it down and this is exactly what this phrase, meaning to let go, refers to. It stems from when Parisian nobles were condemned if they didn't appear in public without an elaborate hairdo, which could take hours to create and were painful to wear, making it wonderfully relaxing to take it down at the end of a long day.

Old-fashioned household tips

If you need to fill a bucket with water from a shallow sink, and you have an open handled dustpan, use this positioned under the tap. The dustpan handle will create a perfect channel to take the water over the sink and into your bucket.

Animal magic

Rats are prolific breeders and brown rats can produce as many as 2,000 offspring a year! They can have as many as 22 young at a time, although the average is around nine. A group of rats is called a mischief, which seems fitting!

Do you remember?

Space hoppers

The secret behind hours of fun in the garden, the space hopper first appeared in the UK in 1969 and quickly bounced off the shelves. It remained a major craze throughout the Seventies and Eighties to be seen bounding around your lawn on one of these.

Recipe of the week

COD LOIN, PROSCIUTTO AND SWEET RED PEPPER SKEWERS

Serves: 4 Prep: 5 mins Cook: 8 mins

500g (1lb 2oz) cod loins, cut into 16 bite-sized chunks
16 slices prosciutto
12 cheese-stuffed sweet peppers in dressing

1 Wrap each piece of fish in a slice of prosciutto. Thread four pieces onto each skewer, alternating with the sweet peppers.
2 Cook on the barbecue with the lid closed for 7-8 mins until the fish has turned white and flakes.
3 Drizzle with dressing from the peppers and serve.
Lakeland

22 SUNDAY

23 MONDAY

24 TUESDAY

25 WEDNESDAY

26 THURSDAY

27 FRIDAY

28 SATURDAY

Blast from the past

THE BOY DONE GOOD

I attended eight schools and hated all of them except for Heathcote Secondary Modern in Stevenage.

Mum took me to my first school in Surrey. We walked there in the rain. We didn't hold hands because boys didn't. Term had already started so I was the only one signing in that day. Mum rang the bell, two huge doors (huge to me, anyway) opened and a man showed us into a lobby. A woman came through a door and tried to hold my hand (but boys didn't hold hands). Mum said: "Go with her, it's okay." We left Mum and the woman, who I found out later was my teacher, took me into a class of what seemed to be hundreds of children. She said: "Tell the class your name."

I said: "Mick. Michael Mannion."

A bigger boy than me shouted: "An Irish Mick!"

I ran out of the class and out of the school. Where was Mum? I remember running and running until I was found by a policeman who took me back to school.

Nine years ago I retired from teaching at a local college so I suppose you could say 'the boy done good'.

Michael Mannion, Anglesey

Where did that come from?

'No spring chicken'

In New England, chicken farmers typically sold their produce in the spring as chickens born in springtime generated better earnings than those that survived the winter. However, sometimes a farmer would sneak an old bird into his stock and try to sell it for the price of the new chickens to which clever buyers would complain the bird was 'no spring chicken' and the term came to mean anyone past their prime.

Old-fashioned household tips

New dishwashing sponges tend to be far larger than necessary. Cutting them in half before use means you only use what you need, and it will dry quicker, harbouring fewer mould-causing bacteria and take up less room by your sink.

Animal magic

Kangaroo offspring are born very early – the equivalent of seven weeks for a human baby. Around the size of a bee, blind and hairless, the joey crawls into its mother's pouch, where it immediately begins feeding off its mother's milk and will spend the next six months or so developing.

Do you remember?

Jackie magazine

Whether you loved the Cathy and Claire problem pages or the pull-out posters of heartthrobs (David Cassidy was a particular favourite), Jackie was the must-have teenage magazine of the Sixties and Seventies, selling well over 600,000 copies at its peak.

Recipe of the week

SPANISH TAPAS PIZZA

Serves: 2 Prep: 15 mins Cook: 30 mins

1 garlic clove, chopped
Olive oil
1 jar passata
Handful of chopped basil leaves
Ready-made pizza dough (try Jus-Rol or Northern Dough Co)
½ red onion sliced into rings
Manchego cheese, grated
Handful of olives
1 small red pepper

1 Preheat your oven to 200°C/400°F/Gas Mark 6. Place pizza stone or baking tray inside to warm up.
2 Fry the garlic in a little oil then add the passata, chopped basil and season. Simmer for 15-20 mins.
3 Roll the dough out onto a lightly floured surface and shape into a circle. You want it to be as thin as possible.
4 Remove the pizza stone or tray from the oven and carefully place your dough on top.
5 Spread a few spoonfuls of the tomato sauce over the base followed by the onion, cheese, olives and red pepper.
6 Cook in the oven for 10-15 mins until crisp and brown.
recipes.uuni.net

29 SUNDAY

30 MONDAY

1 TUESDAY

2 WEDNESDAY

3 THURSDAY

4 FRIDAY

5 SATURDAY

Blast from the past

MUD PIES FOR PUDDING

As a child I was happy in my own little world of make-believe. There was an empty shed in our garden which I had as my own little house. I had boxes for a table and chairs. I collected stones for potatoes, leaves for cabbage, twigs for carrots and pieces of wood for meat. Mum would make me a tiny pot of tea for my tea set and I made mud pies for puddings.

On some days I was more of a tomboy. I made bows and arrows, climbed the only tree in our garden and pretended I was Robin Hood. On wet days, I would get my post office set out or play bus conductors on the stairs.

My mother insisted I play outdoors in nice weather. I was often enjoying myself out in the garden when the elderly lady next door would pop her head over the fence to tell me I should take all my toys in because it was going to rain, so I did. That got me into big trouble with Mum as she told me not to be so daft and not to listen to Mrs Walsh!

The photo shows me (on the left) with my friend Carol.

Evelyn Downs via email

Where did that come from?
'Pleased as punch'
Bizarrely, our childhood amusement of watching a Punch and Judy show actually gave birth to this popular saying for being very happy. Whenever Punch killed people – and he went through everyone from his wife to a policeman to the devil – he was incredibly satisfied and would strut with pride, feeling most pleased with himself as the saying, coined in the early 1800s, suggests.

Old-fashioned household tips

If you're a fan of a fresh cob loaf from the baker or making your own farmhouse, then this tip is for you. For fewer crumbs and easy slicing, use a hot knife. Heat your knife in boiling water for a couple of minutes and dry off quickly before slicing your bread.

Animal magic

It's unlikely to come as a surprise that like us some primates, including chimpanzees and gorillas, have their own unique fingerprints. But, did you know that the koala also has its own fingerprints? Their prints are so similar to ours, that it's almost impossible to tell them apart.

Do you remember?

The rag and bone man

Whatever odds and ends we no longer wanted, we'd always save for the rag and bone man when he did his rounds with his pony we loved to fuss. You'll remember the job was immortalised on screen by Steptoe and Son.

Recipe of the week

QUICK BLACKCURRANT JAM

Makes: 1kg Prep: 30 mins Cook: 10 mins

500g (1lb 2oz) blackcurrants
750g (1lb 10oz) granulated sugar
Few drops of vanilla essence
Juice 1 lemon
½ bottle of Certo (liquid pectin)

1 Remove currants from stalks and place in a pan with the sugar, vanilla essence and lemon juice. Stir once or twice and leave in a warm place to soften for 15 mins.
2 Bring the pan of fruit and currants slowly to the boil to make sure the sugar has completely dissolved. Stir only once or twice, then allow to bubble gently for 5 mins.
3 Remove from the heat and pour in the pectin, boil again gently for 5 mins.
4 When the jam has cooled slightly, stir again and spoon into sterilised jars.
www.berryworld.com

6 SUNDAY

7 MONDAY

8 TUESDAY

9 WEDNESDAY

10 THURSDAY

11 FRIDAY

12 SATURDAY

Blast from the past

THE CATERING CORPS

In October 1974, the girls I taught decided it was time for me to get married as they had seen me and Bob together. In November Bob and I became engaged and a group of girls began planning the wedding which was to take place the following May.

We wanted it to be a quiet wedding with a reception at a cousin's house. I asked the girls if they would do the catering. They consulted magazines and got their cookery teacher involved. Excitement grew and the chattering stopped whenever I appeared. The three-tier cake was created in the cookery room along with cakes and pastries for the wedding breakfast. There was a last-minute hitch when their cookery teacher had an accident, but she sent instructions from her hospital bed and another teacher stepped in to supervise.

On our big day, the church was full and a smiling vicar greeted us. Afterwards, the 'caterers' sped away to await the guests at the reception. When everyone arrived at the house they beheld a feast. The centrepiece was the cake displayed on my grandmother's embroidered tablecloth. The young ladies were there to assist and replenish empty plates and their achievement was applauded by all.   **Priscilla Odell, Hampton**

Where did that come from?

'To run amok'

Meaning to go wild, this saying comes from Malaysia where 'amok' (sometimes spelled amuck or amuco) meant a murderous frenzy or rage. Some say this state of going crazy derived from them taking opium while some people of Malay culture said this was caused by an evil spirit entering a person to make them want to kill others and cause mayhem.

Old-fashioned household tips

A sticky iron can ruin your clothes, leaving black marks on your white shirts and catching on delicate fabrics. Running a warm iron backwards and forwards on a piece of paper sprinkled with salt will help remove any sticky residue.

Animal magic

Octopuses have three hearts, one to pump blood through its organs and the other two to pump blood through its gills. When the octopus swims, the heart which pumps to the organs is inactive, so it tires quickly, which is why octopuses prefer to crawl, rather than swim.

Do you remember?

Fire companion sets

In the days when many of us had a real fire at home, there'd always be the trusty companion set on the side with a poker, roller, shovel and brush to keep the fires that warmed our freezing houses going for as long as possible.

Recipe of the week

BAKED SAUSAGES WITH NEW POTATOES, SPINACH AND ROASTED CHERRY TOMATOES

Serves: 2 Prep: 10 mins Cook: 20 mins

1 tbsp oil, for frying
4-6 good quality Cumberland sausages
150g (5oz) pre-cooked new potatoes, halved
3 tbsp honey mustard
300g (10oz) baby spinach
Large bunch of cherry tomatoes on the vine
2 slices of sourdough bread
Salted butter, to serve

1 Heat the oil in a pan over a medium heat. Add the sausages, and fry for 10-12 mins until evenly browned.
2 Add the halved new potatoes and fry until they soften and begin to brown. Spoon in the honey mustard and stir to coat the potatoes and sausages.
3 Add a large handful of baby spinach to the pan. Reduce the heat and let the spinach wilt.
4 Drizzle the cherry tomatoes with a little olive oil. Season with salt and pepper, then place under a medium grill for 3-5 mins. Season.
5 Toast and butter a slice of sourdough and serve alongside the sausages and vegetables.

www.jonesandsonsdalston.com

13 SUNDAY

14 MONDAY

15 TUESDAY

16 WEDNESDAY

17 THURSDAY

18 FRIDAY

19 SATURDAY

Blast from the past

STILL BEST BUDDIES

This photo of me and my 'best buddy', Vera, was taken outside the Harrington Hotel in London in 1996. I had won a weekend there in a competition. The two of us have been friends since we were teenagers when we shared a love of dancing at the South Parade pier ballroom in Southsea.

We both married Navy chaps from Staffordshire (although they didn't know each other before marrying us!) and our first babies were born in 1954, seven days apart. Our second babies were born four months apart and there was two months between our third babies. We have lots of happy memories of pushing prams, bringing up our children and supporting one another through the tough times.

When our children were grown up we worked for many years as nursing auxilliaries at St Mary's maternity unit in Portsmouth which we loved. We also shared the same driving instructor and passed our test first time. There have been times in our lives when we lived far apart, but letters flew back and forth.

Now in our 80s, we are both widowed and as Vera lives close by I am able to visit her often. Our affection for each other is as strong as ever.
Wendy Nash, Southsea

Where did that come from?
'Hold a candle'
This phrase used when someone compares badly to someone else who is considered a known authority comes from the days when apprentices were expected to literally hold a candle so their more experienced colleagues could see what they were doing. If you couldn't even hold a candle, you were lower than an apprentice and considered of incredibly inferior status.

Old-fashioned household tips

You can often be put off buying a garment that is 'Dry Clean Only' – but remember it's only a recommendation, you can save on bills by cleaning them at home. Lightly soiled clothes can be brushed with a soft bristle brush then hung outside on a breezy day to freshen them.

Animal magic

Ever wondered why you don't see snails during the winter months? Well snails hibernate. They burrow under leaves and soil and cover the opening of their shells with a layer of mucus to keep them cosy when the temperature drops.

Do you remember?

Ovaltine

Mum's favourite bedtime remedy, we were often tucked up with a mug of this malt extract drink. The Beverley sisters played their part in Ovaltine's popularity when their Ovaltineys' advertising jingle became one of the most successful of the era.

Recipe of the week

PUMPKIN AND GRUYÉRE CHEESE TARTS

Serves: 8 Prep: 5 mins Cook: 35 mins

1 pack Jus-Rol shortcrust pastry
3cm grated chunk Parmesan (or vegetarian Parmesan)
5 eggs
5 egg yolks
½ large can of tinned pumpkin
500ml (1pt) double cream
Salt, pepper and nutmeg to season
250g (9oz) Gruyère cheese, cubed, set a few aside

1 Preheat the oven to 180°C/350°F/Gas Mark 4.
2 Turn the pastry onto a floured surface and roll out to a thickness of approx. 4mm (¼in). Cut pastry circles and line eight 12cm (4½in) tartlet tins. Place a layer of greaseproof paper in each, add a few baking beans, bake for 15 mins, remove the paper then allow to cool.
3 When cool, sprinkle the Parmesan into the pastry cases. Mix the remaining filling ingredients together and pour into the cases. Cook for 30 mins, sprinkle the reserved Gruyère cubes on the top and cook for a further 5 mins.
Lakeland

20 SUNDAY

21 MONDAY

22 TUESDAY

23 WEDNESDAY

24 THURSDAY

25 FRIDAY

26 SATURDAY

Blast from the past

SEW FAR, SO GOOD

Unlike my mother who used to knit beautiful Fair Isle patterns, I never mastered the art of knitting. I did better at sewing which I learned at the convent school I attended. Sister Constantine took the class for sewing lessons. Strangely enough, we were only taught to sew aprons!

Throughout my schooldays I sewed lots of aprons. They were already cut out and we had to sew bias binding on the raw edges. We used a running stitch to hold the bias binding in place before turning over the edges and hemming them with a neater stitch. When I was older, we had a different teacher who taught us how to use a sewing machine. My downfall was trying to thread the needle on the machine but eventually I did master it.

As a way of encouraging me, my mother let me use her sewing machine - a hand model as there were no electric ones then. This gave me the confidence later on in life to join a sewing group at an evening class. With a little assistance, I made a two-piece costume. I also made dresses for my daughter when she was little.

Sheila Mills, Minehead

Where did that come from?

'Hair of the dog that bit you'

In medieval times it was believed if you were bitten by a dog, you could be cured of rabies by applying a potion containing hair from the dog that bit you. In 1641 this phrase was first applied to drink, meaning although alcohol may be to blame for a hangover (as the dog was for rabies) a small glass of the same will paradoxically act as cure.

Old-fashioned household tips

It can be a real pain when you break eggs and a piece of the shell drops in; you can spend ages chasing it around a bowl. The best tool for scooping that errant piece out is a larger piece of eggshell - it'll act like a magnet and attract any small bits of shell in seconds.

Animal magic

Spider silk is so durable that it's the strongest natural fibre and relative to weight it's stronger than steel. Amazingly spiders can produce more than one type of silk. Made from protein they create different silks for different purposes, including webs, traps and even shelters.

Do you remember?

Clackers
The cause of many a thumbnail injury, these two balls of plastic on a piece of string provided hours of amusement in the Sixties and Seventies. Unsurprisingly, the name came from the clacking sound they made as they banged against each other.

Recipe of the week

TOMATO AND BUTTERNUT SQUASH LASAGNE

Serves: 6 Prep: 20 mins Cook: 1 hr 35 mins

2kg (4lb 4oz) butternut squash
1 tbsp olive oil
1 onion, chopped
1½ tbsp chopped fresh oregano
2 cloves garlic, crushed
800g (1lb 7oz) can chopped tomatoes
9 sheets dried lasagne
500g (1lb 2oz) white sauce
25g (1oz) Parmigiano Reggiano, or vegetarian alternative

1 Preheat the oven to 180°C/350°F/Gas Mark 4. Peel the squash then halve, discard the seeds and cut into 1cm (½in) pieces.
2 Gently fry the onion and squash in the olive oil for 10 mins, stirring frequently, until the squash is beginning to colour. Add the oregano, garlic and tomatoes and cook gently for 5 mins.
3 Spoon a quarter of the butternut squash mixture into a baking dish and spread in a thin layer. Cover with 3 lasagne sheets, breaking them to fit where necessary. Spoon over another quarter of the squash mixture and dot with about a third of the white sauce. Add another 3 lasagne sheets then half the remaining squash mixture. Arrange the rest of the lasagne sheets on top and spread with the remaining squash mixture. Top with the rest of the white sauce, spreading it to cover the filling.
4 Scatter over the cheese and bake for 50-60 mins until the top is golden and bubbling.
Waitrose

27 SUNDAY

28 MONDAY

29 TUESDAY

30 WEDNESDAY

31 THURSDAY

1 FRIDAY

2 SATURDAY

Blast from the past

A TWINKLE IN HER EYES

This photo of my grandmother with my father (holding his Patrol Sleigh toy) was taken in 1918. Her name was Gertrude Evelyn Mallonek and she was born in London in 1890. By the time this picture was taken she was a ward sister at a hospital in Kent, working with

shell-shocked soldiers. My grandfather was one of the doctors who believed the shell-shocked were not cowards but people who were psychologically damaged. He died when my father was six. During the Second World War my grandmother was the matron of a hospital for similarly afflicted patients.

She lived with us until I was ten, then again from when I was 16 until she died in 1972. I was intrigued by the twinkle in her blue eyes – and her corset! I remember her as a source of buttery mints, a ready audience for my embarrassing 'ballet' performances and a help with confusing homework.

Her German background was never mentioned, but later I found a bankbook from Kelbra, near Leipzig, where she had apparently spent her summer holidays with her own grandmother. There must have been so much more about my grandmother that we never learned.

Julia Newsome, Cumbria

Where did that come from?

'As happy as Larry'

It turns out cheery Larry is most likely to be Australian or New Zealander as the phrase comes from these parts of the world. One possibility is that he's the Australian boxer Larry Foley who never lost a fight (making him pretty jolly we'd imagine). Or else Larry could be a derivation of the slang term 'larrikin' meaning a rough type or hooligan.

Old-fashioned household tips

Old newspapers make great weed killer. Water the ground that has weeds, lay the newspaper on top and around the plants you want to keep and give the newspaper a good soaking with water and cover with about 7cm (3in) of mulch. This will feed the soil and starve the weeds beneath.

Animal magic

A bat is the only mammal that can fly. The world's biggest bat is the Giant Golden-Crowned Flying Fox, with a wingspan that can reach 1.5m. The world's smallest bat is the Kitti's Hog-Nosed or bumblebee bat, with a body that's just 1-1.3in in length.

Do you remember?

Paraffin heaters

With no central heating at home, most of us had no choice but to get a paraffin heater in our bedrooms. It possibly wasn't always the safest option and they had a smell that made us choke, but at least they meant we didn't freeze in winter.

Recipe of the week

PUMPKIN SCONES

Serves: 8 Prep: 15 mins Cook: 20 mins

260g (9oz) plain flour
75g (3oz) light or dark brown sugar
½ tsp ground ginger
½ tsp ground cinnamon
1 tsp baking powder
½ tsp baking soda
¼ tsp salt
113g (4oz) unsalted butter, chilled and cubed
50g (2oz) raisins
120ml (4½ fl oz) buttermilk
120g (4½oz) can tinned or fresh pumpkin
1 tsp vanilla extract
1 egg

1 Preheat the oven to 200°C/400°F/Gas Mark 6. In a bowl, mix together the flour, sugar, spices, baking powder and soda and salt. Using a knife or pastry blade, cut the butter into the flour mix until it resembles coarse breadcrumbs, stir in the raisins.
2 In a separate bowl, mix together the buttermilk, pumpkin and vanilla; add to the flour mixture, then mix until the dough just comes together. Transfer to a lightly floured surface and knead lightly.
3 Divide into 8 portions, pat gently to about 4cm (1½in) thick rounds; place scones onto a baking sheet and brush the tops with beaten egg. Bake for about 20 mins or until golden and a toothpick inserted into the middle comes out clean. Transfer to a wire rack to cool.
Lakeland

3 SUNDAY

4 MONDAY

5 TUESDAY

6 WEDNESDAY

7 THURSDAY

8 FRIDAY

9 SATURDAY

Blast from the past

A COMMUNITY CHOIR

I am very proud of this photo of my son, Mark, taken outside Buckingham Palace when he was invited to the Queen's garden party in recognition of his services to the community.

Twenty-six years ago he set up a choir at his local church which soon became a community choir. It welcomed anyone who wanted to join, regardless of their faith and ability. Over the years the choir has gone from strength to strength, performing at various venues.

For four nights every December the choir puts on concerts at the local parish hall when Mark encourages the children from the village to join in. They have a lot of fun dressing up in the costumes provided and some of the youngsters are given solos which boosts their confidence.

I am told by members of the choir that rehearsals are the highlight of their week as Mark makes them so much fun, and they also appreciate the social aspect and sense of belonging that it gives them. The money raised from the concerts goes to benefit local good causes and charities.

Sylvia Thompson, Dinas Powys

Where did that come from?

'Bring home the bacon'

Meaning to earn money for your family, it's thought this saying goes back to the 1100s in Great Dunnow in Essex where the local church would award a side of bacon to any man who could honestly say he hadn't argued with his wife for a year and a day. Any such man was considered a role model and given the bacon to take home.

Old-fashioned household tips

A drop of milk mixed in with your grated cheese will ensure your Welsh rarebit, croque monsieur or just plain cheese on toast is light and fluffy not tough and leathery.

Animal magic

An adult hedgehog has between 5000-7000 spines, but baby hedgehogs, or hoglets, are born with a protective membrane covering their tiny white prickles. Just below the skin, these spines start to appear within just a few hours after birth and are eventually replaced with tough adult spines.

Do you remember?

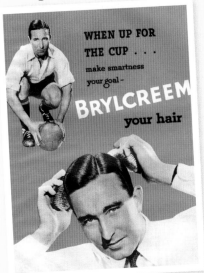

WHEN UP FOR THE CUP . . .

make smartness your goal –

BRYLCREEM your hair

Brylcreem

Our brothers and boyfriends couldn't get enough of this male hair-styling cream, even if we did go mad when they leant against the sofa backs and left a horrible stain. Giving a sleek and sophisticated look, Ronald Reagan was one of its most famous fans.

Recipe of the week

TOFFEE APPLE TART

Serves: 6 Prep: 20 mins Cook: 30 mins

A little melted butter
8 sheets of filo pastry
397g (14oz) tin of dulce de leche
2 apples, peeled, cored and sliced
2 tbsp caster sugar
20g (¾oz) flaked almonds

1 Preheat oven to 200°C/400°F/Gas Mark 6.
2 Brush the inside of a loose-bottom 20cm cake tin with a little melted butter. Take the filo pastry, brush one sheet with melted butter and lay another on top, slightly offsetting the corners. Repeat with the remaining filo pastry sheets.
3 Line the cake tin with the filo stack, allowing the edges of the pastry to hang over the edge. Spread the dulce de leche all over the base of the pastry.
4 Arrange the apple slices over the top in circles. Scrunch the over-hanging pastry over the top of the apples. Brush over with a little butter, sprinkle with sugar and flaked almonds and bake in the oven for 25-30 mins.
www.pinkladyapples.co.uk

10 SUNDAY

11 MONDAY

12 TUESDAY

13 WEDNESDAY

14 THURSDAY

15 FRIDAY

16 SATURDAY

Blast from the past

THE BEST OF FRIENDS

My friend Liz and I met when I was five and she was three years older. We lived in the same street in Leamington Spa. Liz loved coming to our house as her mother was very houseproud and her father quite strict compared with my more relaxed parents.

My parents were into healthy eating and it seemed to me we only ate food that was 'brown' - rice, flour, bread and sugar. I loved to go round to Liz's house and be given white sliced bread and strawberry jam. Bliss!

It was an emotional day when my family left for East Sussex for my father's new job. We promised to write and visit each other as often as we could and vowed that when we got married we would be each other's bridesmaids. We did keep in touch and went on holiday together to Butlin's at Minehead - our first time away without our parents.

We kept our vow. When Liz moved to Germany and married Tom, a captain in the US army, I flew over to be her bridesmaid. In 1978 when I married Alan, Liz came to be my matron of honour (she is next to me in the photo).
Fiona Rouse, Egham

Where did that come from?

'Goody two shoes'
This comes from a Christian retelling of the story of Cinderella called The History of Goody Two-Shoes published in 1765. Well before the idiom got its more negative connotations of describing someone who is over-virtuous, in this tale Goody Two Shoes is a poor orphan who only has one shoe but is given two by a rich man as a reward for being such a good person.

Old-fashioned household tips

Looking for a way to keep your bathroom mirrors, glasses and even car windscreens fog free? When cleaning them add a little squirt of shaving foam to your cloth. This will form a protective layer on the glass preventing them from fogging in the future.

Animal magic

On land wallabies and kangaroos can only move their hind legs together, which is why they use a hopping motion to move around. In water, however, they can kick them independently and are excellent swimmers.

Do you remember?

Andy Pandy

He lived in a picnic basket with friends Teddy and Looby Loo and we loved him ever since he popped on screen in 1950. Our favourite bit was joining in at the end as they sang 'Time to go home, Andy is waving goodbye'.

Recipe of the week

SQUASH, MUSHROOM & HAM PITHIVIER

Serves: 6 Prep: 15 mins Cook: 35 mins

1 butternut squash, peeled, deseeded, halved and sliced
30g (1oz) dried porcini mushrooms
100g (4oz) mascarpone
1 tbsp wholegrain mustard
500g (1lb 2oz) block puff pastry
120g (4oz) pack ham, roughly torn
1 medium free-range egg, beaten

1 Preheat the oven to 200°C/400°F/Gas Mark 6. Cook the squash in boiling water for 5 mins until just tender. Drain and cool. Meanwhile, soak the mushrooms in boiling water for 5 mins, then drain and chop.
2 Mix the mascarpone, mustard and mushrooms together and season well.
3 Roll out one third of the pastry to a 26cm (10in) square, spread one third of the mascarpone mixture over it, leaving a 2cm (¾in) border and place on a baking tray. Layer up with the squash, ham and spoonfuls of the remaining mascarpone, seasoning as you go.
4 Roll out the remaining pastry to a 28cm (11in) square and place on top of the filling. Wet the edges of the base pastry and fold over to seal.
5 Brush the pastry with the beaten egg and bake for 35 minutes until golden.

Waitrose

17 SUNDAY

18 MONDAY

19 TUESDAY

20 WEDNESDAY

21 THURSDAY

22 FRIDAY

23 SATURDAY

Blast from the past

A FAMILY AT WAR

When my father was called up to serve in the Royal Artillery in the Second World War my mother had this photo of us taken at the Dubarry Studio in Birmingham. It was placed in my father's cigarette case so that every time he opened it he knew we were with him.

It was a sad time. I was only a toddler when he went away so my first memory of him is when he came home on leave. When his leave ended he never wanted us to go to the station with him but preferred us to say our goodbyes at home. I remember watching him walk up the road with his haversack on his back. My mother was in tears and to comfort her I said: "I'll look after you, Mummy."

On another occasion we had arranged to spend Christmas with my grandmother when we received a telegram. In those days, a telegram often meant bad news but this one was to say that my father had some leave and would be home for Christmas. My mother had to dash to the shops to see if she could buy a turkey at the last minute!

Pauline Downes, Smethwick

Where did that come from?

'A load of codswallop'

Meaning nonsense, it's thought the word codswallop came about when a man called Hiram Codd patented a bottle for fizzy drinks that had a marble in the neck to keep the bottle shut by pressure of the gas. At the same time, wallop was a slang term for beer and soon after Codd's wallop came to be used as a derogatory term for weak or gassy beer.

Old-fashioned household tips

Non-colourfast clothes particularly new dark jeans will gradually fade with washing and may also bleed onto other garments. To make clothes colourfast, add a cup of vinegar and ¼ cup of salt to 1½ gallons (7 litres) of cold water. Soak your clothes in the solution overnight, then rinse and then wash as usual.

Animal magic

As well as colour changing abilities chameleon's have an impressive tongue, which is on average twice the length of its body. In humans that would be like having a tongue that was ten feet long! Their tongues project forward with such a powerful force that they're able to reach their prey in just 0.07 seconds. Talk about fast food!

Do you remember?

Frozen milk bottles

In the harsh winters of the Fifties and Sixties it was common to head to our doorstep to collect the milk only to find the whole thing was frozen and the cream erupting out of the top, meaning we couldn't even enjoy a warming cup of tea!

Recipe of the week

MACARONI CHEESE

Serves: 4 Prep: 15 mins Cook: 40 mins

300g (10½oz) macaroni
30g (1oz) flour
30g (1oz) low-fat margarine
600ml (1pt) soya milk
150g (5oz) reduced-fat cheddar
30g (1oz) Parmesan cheese
70g (3oz) broccoli florets
70g (3oz) cauliflower florets
40g (1½ oz) wholemeal breadcrumbs
1 pinch cayenne pepper
Salt and pepper to taste

1 Preheat oven to 160°C/350°F/Gas Mark 4.
2 Melt the margarine in a saucepan, remove from the heat and stir in the flour. Return to the heat and gradually add the soya milk.
3 Grate the cheese and add to the sauce. Heat until the cheese has melted and the sauce has a nice thick smooth consistency. Season to taste.
4 Meanwhile, cook the macaroni according to the instructions (usually 10-12 mins). When cooked, stir into the sauce along with the cauliflower and broccoli florets. Add mixture to a baking dish.
5 Mix the breadcrumbs with the grated Parmesan and the cayenne pepper and sprinkle on top of the dish. Cook for 35-40 mins.
Alpro

24 SUNDAY

25 MONDAY

26 TUESDAY

27 WEDNESDAY

28 THURSDAY

29 FRIDAY

30 SATURDAY

Blast from the past

CHRISTMAS AFLOAT

As a surprise for his 65th birthday and retirement, my husband and I spent Christmas 1997 sailing down the Rhine on the M S Diana.

When Kapitan Jean Bowalda spotted my husband videoing me beside his ship, I explained that my name was also Diana and he invited us up on the bridge to meet his wife. We had a wonderful time with amazing three-course meals, music and dancing every evening and a fun-loving crew of many nationalities.

On Christmas Day, the captain dressed up as Father Christmas and the first mate, disguised as a reindeer, presented us with stollen and small bottle of wine. The captain even sent for Christmas crackers to be delivered 'for the English'.

In Cologne the shop windows were lit up with decorations but we were amused to see in a baker's shop a family of mice happily eating their way through the display of bread!

The highlight of our holiday was a visit to Siegfried's mechanical cabinet museum, the first collection of automated instruments in Germany. We were invited to link arms, dance and sing before being presented with a blue and gold mug filled with Gluhwein.
Diana Manning, Campbeltown

Where did that come from?
'Happy as a sand boy'
In Bristol, there were pubs where fine sand from sea caves would be strewn on the floor to soak up any spillages. The lads who would go to the beach to collect the sand for this purpose were paid partly by drink so were usually very happy and merry, like the meaning of this phrase today.

Old-fashioned household tips

To prevent large items of furniture (or ornaments) from scratching your flooring, cut 4 thin slices of cork from a wine bottle and superglue it under the corners.

Animal magic

One of the fastest animals on the planet is the peregrine falcon. This magnificent bird was once declining in population but is now on the rise. Traditionally found nesting in the Highlands and on coastal cliffs, this beautiful bird of prey has been spotted in some unusual nesting sites including Derby Cathedral and the BT Tower in Birmingham.

Do you remember?

Tin baths by the fire

With no proper indoor plumbing, some of us will remember splashing around in the front room for the weekly bath – usually on a Sunday. Sometimes family members would take it in turns to have a bath with the water saved to wash clothes later.

Recipe of the week

CREAM OF MUSHROOM SOUP

Serves: 4 Prep: 40 mins Cook: 25 mins

50g (2oz) Porcini mushrooms
1 knob of butter
1 banana shallot, finely diced
2 cloves garlic crushed
1 sprig of thyme
450g (1lb) mixed mushrooms roughly chopped (chestnut, oyster and button)
1 litre (1½pt) of chicken or vegetable stock
200ml (7fl oz) Alpro Soya Single or single cream (plus a little extra for garnish)
Handful chopped parsley

1 Pour 100ml (4fl oz) of boiling water over the porcini mushrooms and leave to soak.
2 Melt the butter in a large, heavy-based pan over a medium heat. Add the shallot, garlic, thyme and mushrooms. Continue cooking for 5 mins until the mushrooms have reduced in volume by about half. Add in the stock and porcini mushrooms along with the soaking liquid.
3 Continue cooking for a further 20 mins before adding in the cream and blitzing with a hand blender.
4 Serve with a drizzle of cream and a sprinkle of parsley.
Alpro

1 SUNDAY

2 MONDAY

3 TUESDAY

4 WEDNESDAY

5 THURSDAY

6 FRIDAY

7 SATURDAY

Blast from the past

FAMILY FESTIVITY

This is one of my favourite photos of my mum
and dad taken at Christmas in the Eighties.
Some of my happiest memories of my
childhood are of Christmas as my parents would
make it such a special time, despite having
little money. When we were small, Dad made
many presents for us such as garages and zoo
enclosures for my brother and an amazing doll's
house, complete with furniture, for me. He also
made me a doll's cot while Mum knitted clothes
for my doll. My beautiful, kind mum managed
to amass thoughtful gifts that we treasured.

By the time this picture was taken, my brother
and I were both married, but we always went to
my parents for Boxing Day. It was a lovely family
get-together when Mum would put on one of her
legendary teas consisting of various sandwiches,
home-baked savouries, cakes and a trifle. It
wasn't long before my two children joined the
Boxing Day party and after tea we used to play
games in the front room which was reserved for
Christmas and special occasions.

Looking at old photos brings back such
happy memories.
Sally Burton-Pye, Cromer

Where did that come from?
'To win hands down'
To do something without any great effort,
this phrase comes from horse racing where a
jockey who is winning very comfortably does
not need to even use a whip to get to the end.
He can therefore ride to the finishing line and
win with his hands down, loosened on the
reins instead of up bearing a whip.

Old-fashioned household tips

To make your own garden flower-scented air freshener, fill a spray bottle with 240ml (8fl oz) tap water 8 drops lavender essential oil, 5 drops geranium essential oil, 4 drops grapefruit essential oil and 2 tbsp of vodka. Shake well and spray.

Animal magic

The pygmy shrew is the smallest mammal in Britain with a body length of 40-60mm and a tail length of around 32-46mm. Due to its tiny stature, it has a very fast metabolism, which means that just two hours after eating it's hungry again.

Do you remember?

Raleigh Choppers

A revolutionary new style of bike with its ape hanger handle bars and long padded saddle, the Raleigh Chopper was on top of every child's Christmas list in the Seventies. Inspired in design by the Chopper motorcycle, it became a cultural icon of the era.

Recipe of the week

PORK, SAGE AND CRANBERRY STUFFING

Serves: 8 Prep: 15 mins Cook: 30 mins

454g (1lb) pack sausagemeat
3 shallots, finely chopped
20g (¾ oz) pack fresh sage, leaves only, finely chopped
75g (3oz) fresh cranberries, chopped
75g (3oz) fresh breadcrumbs
8 rashers smoked streaky bacon

1 Preheat the oven to 200°C/400°F/Gas Mark 6. Mix together the sausagemeat, shallots, sage, cranberries and breadcrumbs. Season.
2 Stretch the bacon with the back of a knife and cut in half. Use to line 8 holes of a muffin tin and fill with the sausagemeat. Wrap the ends of the bacon over.
3 Bake for 25 mins until thoroughly cooked. Cool slightly, then upturn onto a baking tray and grill for 2-3 mins. Serve with roast turkey or an alternative meat.
Waitrose

8 SUNDAY

9 MONDAY

10 TUESDAY

11 WEDNESDAY

12 THURSDAY

13 FRIDAY

14 SATURDAY

Blast from the past

LET IT SNOW!

This is my son, Richard, aged about five when we had a lot of snow in the Midlands. He is in his 40s now and probably doesn't remember how much snow we used to get every year.

At the back of our house we had a large open space with a huge hill leading to a tunnel. All the children used to gather there with their sledges and play until it grew dark. The object was to see if you could reach the tunnel and glide through it. The adults also enjoyed the fun – me being one of them!

My son and daughter were fascinated that year by the amount of snow blocking the lane near our house. It was so deep that it was up to the tops of the hedges and buried underneath we found two cars completely covered by snow. Luckily, there was no-one inside and the vehicles had to be dug out and the lane cleared before they could be moved.

I love the snow, but now living in Cornwall we don't get any, and not much frost either.

Mrs C Davies, Wadebridge

Where did that come from?

'Before you can say Jack Robinson'

While there's lots of speculation about who Jack is, one theory is that it wasn't originally Jack but John Robinson who between 1660 and 1679 was the commanding officer at the Tower of London who had a reputation for chopping off people's heads with amazing speed. Another possible Jack Robinson is a 19th Century Englishman known to change his mind a lot meaning you had to be quick to catch him in a decision.

Old-fashioned household tips

If your curtain rings tend to get stuck when you open and close the curtains, give the pole a coat of wax polish, this will make your curtains easier to draw and less likely to suffer damage.

Animal magic

Wild turkeys can actually fly and even fly pretty fast, albeit for not very long or far! Domestic turkeys are commercially bred and are too heavy to fly, whereas wild turkeys are lighter so able to get airborne.

Do you remember?

Etch-a-sketch

There was always something magical about Etch-a-Sketch. Twist a couple of knobs and miraculously a drawing appears. Then turn it upside down and a quick shake and the whole thing goes. It remains a popular toy even today, more than 60 years after its invention.

Recipe of the week

ORANGE CRUMBLE MINCE PIES

Serves: 24 Prep: 35 mins, plus chilling, standing and cooling
Cook: 15 mins

225g (8oz) plain flour, plus extra for rolling
50g (2oz) ground almonds
50g (2oz) caster sugar
125g (4½oz) unsalted butter, chilled and diced
Vanilla seeds scraped from a pod
1 egg yolk
For the orange crumble:
75g (3oz) plain flour
6 tbsp demerara sugar
60g (2½oz) unsalted butter
1 orange, zest
1 tsp mixed spice
800g (1lb 7oz) mincemeat
Icing sugar, for dusting

1 For the pastry, put the flour, almonds, caster sugar, butter and vanilla seeds in a food processor and whizz to form crumbs. Add the egg yolk and 1 tbsp cold water. Pulse until it forms a dough, adding a drop more water if needed. Turn onto your worktop and gently knead until smooth. Wrap in clingfilm and chill for about 30 mins.
2 To make the crumble topping briefly pulse together the flour, demerara sugar, butter, orange zest and mixed spice to a chunky crumble mixture, then set aside.
3 Preheat the oven to 200°C/400°F/Gas Mark 6. Roll out the chilled pastry to the thickness of a £1 coin on a lightly floured surface and cut out 24 rounds using an 8-9cm pastry cutter. Press the rounds into the holes of 2 x 12-hole bun tins and lightly pinch the edges with your fingers for a fluted effect.
4 Divide the mincemeat between the cases and scatter the crumble over the top. Bake for 15 mins, or until golden and crunchy.
5 Once cooled, dust with icing sugar to serve.
Waitrose

15 SUNDAY

16 MONDAY

17 TUESDAY

18 WEDNESDAY

19 THURSDAY

20 FRIDAY

21 SATURDAY

Blast from the past

CHRISTMAS BIKE BUILD

My happiest memories of Christmas when my children were young was 1984. My husband, John and I were a young married couple. Our daughter, Katharine was eight and our son, Jonathan was two. We finally got the excited children in bed late on Christmas Eve. John went to the garage to bring in the large box containing Katharine's new bike. When we opened the box, the bike was in pieces - it had to be built. John then spent four hours building the bike!

We went to bed in the early hours and the children got up at 3.45am on Christmas morning! They loved their toys but Jonathan spent the day playing with the bike box instead of his toys. Maybe I was tired or excited when I was preparing the meal but when my dear Dad carved the turkey for Christmas dinner, he pulled out the giblets still in their bag. It was a Christmas Day we will never forget!
Rosie Sandall, Peterborough

Where did that come from?

'Pull someone's leg'
It might be a matter of joking around with someone these days, but pulling someone's leg initially had far more sinister connotations. When thieves were trying to rob someone they would trip them up and use different instruments to knock them to the ground, literally pulling their leg from beneath them so they could rob them.

Old-fashioned household tips

Baking soda has an assortment of uses around the home. Put some in a small dish and place it on a shelf in your fridge, it'll absorb any nasty niffs. Try putting some on a damp cloth and use to buff away scuffs from hard, lino or tiled floors.

Animal magic

With such big ears, it's probably no surprise that donkeys have pretty good hearing. That isn't their only use though. Donkeys are originally from hot desert areas and their larger ears help to dissipate heat and keep them cool.

Do you remember?

Morecambe and Wise Christmas specials

It wasn't really Christmas until Eric and Ernie gave us a stitch from laughing. From conductor André Previn's hilarious concerto catastrophe to dancing newsreaders dressed up as sailors, their shows were guaranteed comedy gold that went down in history as some of the most memorable sketches ever.

Recipe of the week

TOFFEE AND CRANBERRY PUDDINGS

Serves: 6 Prep: 10 mins Cook: 25-30 mins

110g (4oz) butter
175g (6oz) soft brown sugar
2 eggs
1 tsp vanilla
110g (4oz) wholemeal self-raising flour
50g (2oz) cranberries
For the sauce:
110g (4oz) cranberries
110g (4oz) soft brown sugar
25g (1oz) butter

1 Preheat oven to 180°C/350°F/Gas Mark 4.
2 Cream the butter and sugar together until light and fluffy. Then blend in the eggs, vanilla, flour and cranberries, adding a little milk if necessary.
3 Spoon mixture into lightly greased individual pudding basins. Cover each loosely with a piece of greased baking paper. Place on a baking tray and bake for 25-30 mins until well risen.
4 For the sauce, place cranberries in a saucepan with 4 tbsp water and the sugar and heat gently until cranberries pop and sauce reduces. Stir in butter and simmer until sauce thickens. Turn out puds and pour on a little of the cranberry toffee sauce. Serve with rest of sauce.
Berryworld

22 SUNDAY

23 MONDAY

24 TUESDAY

25 WEDNESDAY

26 THURSDAY

27 FRIDAY

28 SATURDAY

Blast from the past

BEST CHRISTMAS EVER!

I didn't realise it at the time but this is the Christmas that set me on the road for my future career. It was around 1976 and I so clearly remember unwrapping what I think still ranks as one of my favourite gifts - a giant artists' compendium and sketch pad. It was packed with poster paint, coloured pencils, watercolours, brushes, palettes and more... and best of all it was all mine! For me this was heaven. I loved drawing, in fact I was so keen in junior school I would set myself little 'homework projects' such as creating a spotters' guide to garden birds, complete with detailed drawings and descriptions.

Up until this Christmas I'd had the frustration of having to share a box of chewed and broken coloured pencils with my older brother and sister, but now I could let my creativity fly. I spent every spare minute drawing and painting, sketching pets and family members as soon as they sat still. I went on to study art at O'Level and then to art college (much to the confusion and consternation of my careers' advisor). After four years, I graduated as a graphic designer and that's how I made my living for many years. All thanks to my parents choosing to foster my burgeoning creativity.
Lesley Palmer, Leicester

Where did that come from?

'Straight from the horse's mouth'

The only way of getting information from the most reliable source, this saying is said to come from the 1900s when a buyer would determine a horse's true age by examining its teeth. It's also why you shouldn't 'look a gift horse in the mouth', as inspecting a gift too much is considered bad etiquette.

Old-fashioned household tips

If your kitchen scissors or tin opener are a bit blunt, you can sharpen them without needing any special tools. Concertina a length of aluminium foil about half a dozen times. Then cut strips along the length. Alternatively scrunch up a ball of foil and carefully rub along the edges of your scissors.

Animal magic

Reindeers are the only deer where both sexes grow antlers. Natural antler shedding occurs at different times of the year for males and females. Mature males generally lose their antlers in winter, somewhere between November and December, which means Father Christmas probably used an all-female line-up to pull his sleigh.

Do you remember?

Be-Ro Recipe Book

They might be a bit tatty and slightly flour-covered today, but the Be-Ro recipe book has long been a mainstay of our kitchen cupboards, called upon whenever the urge to bake strikes. First produced in 1923, it has since sold more than 38 million copies.

Recipe of the week

MINCEMEAT TRAYBAKE

Makes: 48 Prep: 5 mins Cook: 50-60 mins

For the traybake:
180g (6oz) butter
300g (10½ oz) demerara sugar
Zest of 1 orange
400g (14oz) mincemeat
1 tsp cinnamon
1 large egg, beaten
350g (12oz) self-raising flour
For the topping:
200g (7oz) butter, softened
400g (14oz) icing sugar
1 tsp vanilla extract
100g (4oz) white chocolate, melted
White chocolate shavings
Chopped mixed nuts and fruit

1 Preheat the oven to 180°C/350F/Gas Mark 4.
2 Melt the butter and sugar in a large saucepan over a low heat, stirring well to ensure that the sugar dissolves.
3 Remove from the heat and allow to cool slightly. Add the orange zest, mincemeat, cinnamon and egg. Stir in the flour and mix thoroughly.
4 Pour the mixture into the traybake tin and bake in the centre of the oven for 50-60 mins. Allow to cool in the tin.
5 To make the topping, place the softened butter and half the icing sugar in a bowl and beat until smooth. Add the remaining icing sugar and mix until smooth and creamy, then add the vanilla extract and white chocolate and mix well. Set aside until the traybake has completely cooled.
6 Top the traybake with the buttercream, then decorate with white chocolate shavings and chopped mixed nuts and fruit.

29 SUNDAY

30 MONDAY

31 TUESDAY

1 WEDNESDAY

2 THURSDAY

3 FRIDAY

4 SATURDAY

Blast from the past

WE ELOPED TO GRETNA

This photo was taken in Gretna Green when I was a runaway bride. Unfortunately, the camera was dropped and the only one we managed to save was this one of me in my wedding dress.

In 1955 things were very different from today. I was 17 when my boyfriend, Michael, suggested that we should get married and move into our own place. However, my father said no as I was far too young. In those days you had to have permission from your parents if you wanted to get married before you were 21. There were always stories in the newspapers about couples running away to Gretna Green so that's what Michael and I decided to do. You had to stay for three weeks to get a marriage licence and we managed to find a dear lady to lodge with.

At the time you don't think about the worry your parents go through when they find out. I very much regret this now and when I had my own children it really upset me to think of the distress I caused my family.

However, Michael and I were married for 40 years and I wonder how many runaway brides can say that?

Margaret Harmer, E Sussex

Where did that come from?

'Cost an arm and leg'

The story goes that this phrase came from 18th Century paintings when famous people such as George Washington would have portraits done without certain limbs showing in the picture. This is because having limbs included was said to have cost more to paint and so they simply didn't bother. That's why the phrase today refers to something extremely expensive.

Old-fashioned household tips

Take potatoes out of their plastic bag and store them in a cold, dark place. You can also try putting an apple in with them as they produce ethlylene gas which, while it ripens fruits quickly, actually prevents potatoes from sprouting.

Animal magic

Classed as marine animals, polar bears are powerful swimmers using their front paws as paddles and back paws as rudders. They can reach swimming speeds of 6mph and are capable of swimming for several hours without rest. One female polar bear was tracked swimming non-stop for nearly ten days.

Do you remember?

Tonight...a sparkling Babycham

Babycham

Come every New Year's Eve, we reached to the back of the drinks' cupboard for a little tipple of Babycham. Light, sparkling perry that made us feel fizzy and rather light-headed, it was one of the first alcoholic drinks marketed directly to women.

Recipe of the week

ROAST RUMP OF BEEF WITH GARLIC AND THYME

Serves: 6 Prep: 15 mins + 2 hrs marinating Cook: 40 mins

4 cloves garlic, chopped
½ pack fresh thyme
2 shallots, sliced
3 tbsp olive oil
850g (1lb 9oz) British beef top rump roast
700g (1lb 8oz) sliced and peeled butternut squash

1 Preheat the oven to 200°C/400°F/Gas Mark 6. Mix together the garlic, thyme, sliced shallots, olive oil and seasoning in a shallow dish. Add the beef, turning to coat in the marinade, cover and refrigerate for 1½-2 hrs, turning a couple of times. Remove from the marinade. Add the squash to the leftover marinade and toss to coat.
2 Heat a heavy-duty roasting tin on the hob over a high heat and brown the beef on all sides then transfer the tin to the oven and calculate the cooking time: 20 mins/500g for rare, 25 mins for medium and 30 mins for well done. Cook for the calculated time adding the butternut squash to the tin for the last 40 mins and turn once during cooking.
3 Remove the beef from the oven and transfer to a warm platter. Serve with the roasted butternut squash wedges, Yorkshire pudding and gravy.
Waitrose

2019 year-to-view calendar

JANUARY

M		7	14	21	28	
Tu	1	8	15	22	29	
W	2	9	16	23	30	
Th	3	10	17	24	31	
F	4	11	18	25		
Sa	5	12	19	26		
Su	6	13	20	27		

FEBRUARY

M		4	11	18	25	
Tu		5	12	19	26	
W		6	13	20	27	
Th		7	14	21	28	
F	1	8	15	22		
Sa	2	9	16	23		
Su	3	10	17	24		

MARCH

M		4	11	18	25	
Tu		5	12	19	26	
W		6	13	20	27	
Th		7	14	21	28	
F	1	8	15	22	29	
Sa	2	9	16	23	30	
Su	3	10	17	24	31	

APRIL

M	1	8	15	22	29	
Tu	2	9	16	23	30	
W	3	10	17	24		
Th	4	11	18	25		
F	5	12	19	26		
Sa	6	13	20	27		
Su	7	14	21	28		

MAY

M		6	13	20	27	
Tu		7	14	21	28	
W	1	8	15	22	29	
Th	2	9	16	23	30	
F	3	10	17	24	31	
Sa	4	11	18	25		
Su	5	12	19	26		

JUNE

M		3	10	17	24	
Tu		4	11	18	25	
W		5	12	19	26	
Th		6	13	20	27	
F		7	14	21	28	
Sa	1	8	15	22	29	
Su	2	9	16	23	30	

JULY

M	1	8	15	22	29	
Tu	2	9	16	23	30	
W	3	10	17	24	31	
Th	4	11	18	25		
F	5	12	19	26		
Sa	6	13	20	27		
Su	7	14	21	28		

AUGUST

M		5	12	19	26	
Tu		6	13	20	27	
W		7	14	21	28	
Th	1	8	15	22	29	
F	2	9	16	23	30	
Sa	3	10	17	24	31	
Su	4	11	18	25		

SEPTEMBER

M		2	9	16	23	30
Tu		3	10	17	24	
W		4	11	18	25	
Th		5	12	19	26	
F		6	13	20	27	
Sa		7	14	21	28	
Su	1	8	15	22	29	

OCTOBER

M		7	14	21	28	
Tu	1	8	15	22	29	
W	2	9	16	23	30	
Th	3	10	17	24	31	
F	4	11	18	25		
Sa	5	12	19	26		
Su	6	13	20	27		

NOVEMBER

M		4	11	18	25	
Tu		5	12	19	26	
W		6	13	20	27	
Th		7	14	21	28	
F	1	8	15	22	29	
Sa	2	9	16	23	30	
Su	3	10	17	24		

DECEMBER

M		2	9	16	23	30
Tu		3	10	17	24	31
W		4	11	18	25	
Th		5	12	19	26	
F		6	13	20	27	
Sa		7	14	21	28	
Su	1	8	15	22	29	

RELAX & UNWIND

A class act

Variety is dying – and Vince and Harry are feeling the pinch

The assistant stage manager at the Empire Theatre raised his eyes to the ceiling in a 'here we go again' look as the double act of Harry and Vince came off and walked into the wings, almost knocking him over as they brushed past him and the scantily clad dancers who were waiting to go on.

Harry, the senior of the two could be heard ranting and raving as they made their way down to the dressing rooms. Vince didn't say a word as, for the second time that day, he watched Harry open a bottle of whisky. Not bothering with the nicety of a glass, he proceeded to swig it straight from the bottle.

The two of them had been together for more than 20 years. Harry was well known in the profession for his heavy drinking, which was a constant source of worry to Vince. Recently, he had been hitting the bottle harder than ever - it was the Fifties and throughout the country the death knell was sounding for variety theatres. With the advent of television - since the Queen's Coronation almost every home had one - their demise seemed imminent.

The first house on a Monday night was enough to make a saint turn to drink. "How can I get any response from an audience of 22 people - and 15 of those are complimentary tickets?" Harry complained bitterly, only too aware that like the rest of the cast they were on a percentage of the box office. "And that so-called blinking

comedian didn't help by cutting his act short," he added.

Vince rasped back: "You can't blame him with an audience like that. The way we were going I thought we'd have to cut ours as well."

Harry glared at him. "Okay! Okay! I know what you're going to say next!"

Vince continued accusingly: "You've been guzzling booze for the past 18 years but the smell of whisky on your breath tonight was the worst I've ever known - you almost made ME forget my lines."

"Why don't you change the record?" asked Harry wearily.

"And don't make that old excuse about first-night jitters. It's about time you got over

---

"Vince silently prayed that the second house would be better and that Harry would be sober enough to go on and do his stuff"

---

those by now," Vince responded.

"It's not the first-night jitters, it's the uncertainty of this business that's really getting to me. We can't go on like this for much longer - but how else can we make a living? It's the only thing we know. And admit it, you'd be lost without me."

"Oh yes, I'd miss this eternal bickering, wouldn't I?" Vince responded sarcastically. "And, while we're on the subject, I didn't care for the way that girl dancer was eyeing you up and down - although why she should show an interest in a hopeless alcoholic like you, escapes me."

Harry mimicked him: "And I didn't like the way she eyed you up and down! Oh, dear. No need to panic, it's just a little harmless flirtation - there's no danger of her coming between us."

In spite of their continual arguing, the two performers cared for each other. An affection born out of the mixed fortunes that are inevitable in show business, and years of touring all over the country bound them together.

"There'd better not be," Vince replied from his usual seat in the corner of their dressing room. This was the only career that he'd ever known, the only world in which he felt at home. He liked to think that he and Harry played an important

part in entertaining the great British public. Harry had come from a poor background and the drudgery of manual work had driven him to find a more exciting way of life. He had gone on the stage and after many years of hard slog had eventually hit on a variety act that got star billing.

Looking across at the other half of his double act, Harry commented: "It's time you had a new coat. In fact, I think we should create a completely different image for ourselves."

Vince remained silent; he had

WORDS: BOB BROADFIELD/ILLUSTRATION: KATE DAVIES

heard all this before. Yes, he did need a new costume, the one he had was threadbare, but it would have to wait until better times came along.

Since the bookings for their act had dropped off, they were just about able to make ends meet – although Harry always seemed to find enough money to purchase a bottle of whisky. Vince silently prayed that the second house would be better, and that Harry would be sober enough to go on and do his stuff.

An hour later, the bottle of whisky was almost empty. There was a knock at the door. The call boy chanted: "Overture and beginners, please, Overture and beginners, please."

Harry rushed over to the door. "What's the house like?" he asked, almost pleadingly.

"Looks good," replied the boy. "It's just beginning to fill up."

He was right. The excitement and general hubbub generated by the audience percolated backstage. Their mood of anticipation even permeated the

dingy dressing room. Suddenly Harry's whole demeanour changed. He snapped out of his gloom and became bright and full of resolve.

Turning to Vince, he smacked his hands together and said: "Right, let's go out there and slay 'em." And with that he picked Vince up, sat him in the crook of his arm and carried him out of the dressing room.

Vince remained silent. After all, if you're a ventriloquist's dummy, you don't get much of a say in things.

Two-speed crossword

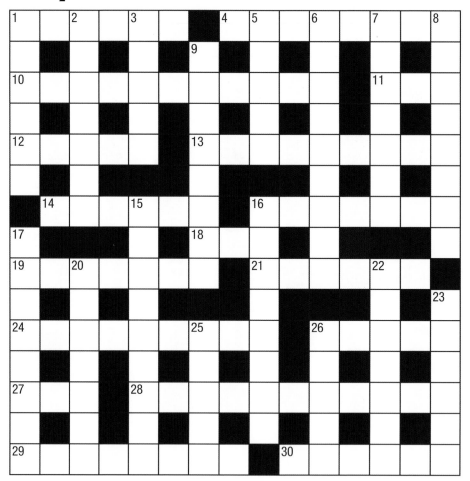

For this puzzle we've provided two sets of clues, each giving the same answers. Quick clues are below and Cryptic to the right. It's a good way to hone your skills, because it gives you two ways to crack the crossword!

ACROSS
1   Recommence (6)
4   Seat of government in the Netherlands (3, 5)
10 MC at a formal meal (11)
11 Indication of a woman's original surname (3)
12 Painter's stand (5)
13 Track or field events (9)
14 Lady in distress? (6)
16 Sailing vessel such as Drake's Golden Hind (7)
18 Day before (3)
19 US drama series starring Glenn Close (7)
21 See 23D
24 Quarter of a city where Cantonese is spoken? (9)
26 Hawaiian farewell (5)
27 Secure with a rope (3)
28 Name adopted by Cassius Clay (8, 3)
29 Begrudged (8)
30 TV-filming room (6)

DOWN
1   Dastardly rogue (6)
2   Port in south Wales (7)
3   Roadside guesthouse (5)
5   Snag (5)
6   High jinks, tomfoolery (9)
7   Authentic (7)
8   Christian service of prayers also called vespers (8)
9   Irons, handcuffs (8)
15 The - - -, classic ghost story by Charles Dickens (6,3)
16 Famed Native American Apache leader (8)
17 Teacher (8)
20 Young ladies (7)
22 Panther (7)
23 & 21A Ian Fleming spy novel (6, 6)
25 Yellowy-brown shade (5)
26 Modify for new circumstances (5)

Puzzles

ACROSS

1 Continue CV (6)
4 Article by Foreign Secretary gives location of International Court of Justice (3, 5)
10 Dinnertime compere putting grilled bread in front of boy (11)
11 Born as pioneers, partly (3)
12 Artist's aid to relieve learner (5)
13 Sports breaking each stilt (9)
14 One of the 20D, perhaps, builds a river barrier in front of English lake (6)
16 Quantity of liquid's taken east in ship (7)
18 First woman among seven (3)
19 Spoils compensation (7)
21 See 23D
24 Jack Nicholson film set in Shanghai? (9)
26 A Spanish greeting about to become a greeting from a different language (5)
27 Draw neckwear (3)
28 Mother eating meat with a surrealist boxer! (8, 3)
29 Now leader's left, Mr Miliband felt bitter (8)
30 Small, flat jewellery for the ear – one ring (6)

DOWN

1 River animal – this one's a rat! (6)
2 Graceful birds seen over half of east Wales's second city (7)
3 Place for a driver to rest before the Spanish check on vehicle's safety (5)
5 Pull up trousers and attack church (5)
6 Production of Equus, maybe, is all fun and games (9)
7 Real trouble for ingénue (7)
8 Regular bird noise – it's heard in the chapel (8)
9 Chaps outside brought up tin fetters (8)
15 Railway worker maligns dreadful article (9)
16 Shout for a jumper given back by round youngster, for example (8)
17 Tutor raced out in confusion (8)
20 Girls: get more than one over without scoring! (7)
22 Mr Sayer's average day with big cat (7)
23 & 21A Unfortunately, Cairo's university holds no adventure for James Bond (6, 6)
25 Mineral rock containing fringes of clayish, earthy pigment (5)
26 Advert on suitable change (5)

Wordsearch 1

Can you find all these food items that can be cooked in the oven?

APPLE	MERINGUE
BISCUIT	PARSNIP
BREAD	PASTIES
CASSEROLE	PIE
CHICKEN	PIZZA
COOKIE	POTATOES
CUPCAKE	QUICHE
FLAPJACK	SCONE
FRUITCAKE	SPONGE
LAMB	TURKEY

```
X M P O T A T O E S P
N R X B S E G Y B B K
E F B U W A P Z I O E
K Y L A M B Z S M G K
C S Z A J O C Z N R A
I R C Q P U R O I E C
H L Z O I J P G N P P
C B R T N S A I G H U
D A E R B E E C V E C
V E H C I U Q M K K A
I M Q Q P I N S R A P
H E A V B L V Z W C F
J R N D H B Z A S T H
E I K O O C P P A I H
F N V G T P A I U U T
I G U W L I S E I R U
R U N E T Z T E U F R
I E A G M J I J S T K
N R C A S S E R O L E
C T H K D T S Y D H Y
```

Were you right? Turn to page 182 for the answers

After the storm

Jealousy is ruining Sara and Lisa's holiday...

The lightning illuminated the untidy room – the beach towels, swimsuit hanging on the door knob, sunglasses discarded on the chest of drawers. Then a loud clap of thunder made Sara jump and move closer to her sleeping husband. She could hear the rain drumming on the roof of the beach house.

The day had been oppressive and stifling. And it wasn't only the weather. Sara reflected on her own earlier behaviour. She knew that she had been immature and sulky, but she blamed her sister. Lisa had burst out with her news, destroying the calm and relaxation of their summer holiday.

Next to Sara, her husband Jeff snored on, oblivious as usual to any disturbances. She kicked him briefly under the sheet but there was no response. He and Lisa's husband had done nothing to settle the argument, refusing to get involved. They were used to the sisters bickering and took no notice, knowing from experience they would soon be friends again.

But, Sara thought, this was different from their usual quarrels. This was something bigger than a missed birthday or some silly misunderstanding. Gradually the rain abated and she drifted off to sleep.

By the morning, the storm had cleared and Sara woke early. Still groggy from her broken night's sleep, she moved slowly around the kitchen before anyone else stirred. The mug of tea in her hands was hot and comforting.

The house was right next to the beach with wide windows looking out on the waves and clear blue sky. It was small and shabbily decorated with an eclectic mix of furniture, but it was the view that sold it to Sara - uninterrupted shades of blue as far as the eye could see.

They had booked the holiday spontaneously after a conversation on the phone. It was a rare treat for the sisters to spend quality time together and Sara had been looking forward to it for months. But instead of a much-needed break from stress and worry, Lisa's news was ruining it all.

Sara finished her tea, picked up her book and sunglasses, and walked across the rickety boardwalk to the beach.

Even though it was early, the sun was scorching. There were few people about. Only some runners, panting and sweaty, braved the heat. Tiny crabs regarded her from their makeshift holes. Sara flicked a few grains of sand at them and they darted back out of sight.

A figure blocked out the sun. Sara squinted up at the silhouette of her sister. Lisa paused for a second then sat next to her, silently fidgeting with the book on her lap.

Eventually, she said: "I'm sorry."

"What for?"

"You know."

"But this was different from their usual quarrels. This was something bigger than a silly misunderstanding"

Sara looked at Lisa who was always the peacemaker, always the one to apologise first. She noticed that her sister's body was changing already, showing curves where there had been straight lines. She said: "Well, it's not as though you could have kept it quiet for ever."

"But I shouldn't have blurted it out like that. I was going to sit down with you, be a bit more sensitive."

"Right."

"It's just that we are so excited."

"I can imagine."

And it was true. She could. Sara remembered all those times when she and Jeff had felt the first buzz of anticipation only to discover they were false alarms. All those 'what if' thoughts, the tentative smiles and the planning. But their hopes were invariably shattered a few days later and eventually brought to an end completely when the doctor confirmed that they couldn't have children.

He'd told them that they could keep trying but they shouldn't expect miracles and suggested considering other options. And now here was her younger sister who hadn't even been trying, who'd once said she didn't really want children, announcing she was 12 weeks pregnant - and had

WORDS: LOUISA DE LANGE/ILLUSTRATION: KATE DAVIES

the fuzzy black-and-white scan photos to prove it.

It was so unfair. Sara wondered whether she was more angry with her sister or with fate itself.

"Do you want to see?" Lisa offered the photos tentatively. Sara took them and held them carefully, knowing how precious they were. Looking closely, she could just about make out a tiny head and hands, and spine curving along the bottom of the picture.

"He's about this big," Lisa said, holding her fingers about six centimetres apart.

"He?"

"Or maybe she," her sister smiled, and shrugged. "We don't know yet, of course, but I can't bear just calling him 'it'. We can't wait, we just want to know!"

"He's going to be beautiful, Lisa," she whispered, handing back the photos. "I know he is."

"Thank you," Lisa said and squeezed her hand. "And you will always be there, won't you? Auntie Sara?"

Sara nodded and looked away, feeling the tears pricking behind her eyes. Auntie. She had never considered that option.

Auntie Sara. Yes, she would always be there, all through his – or her – life. Maybe she and Jeff couldn't have children of their own (although they hadn't ruled out the other options suggested by the doctor) but she would still be Auntie Sara.

She sat back in her chair and raised her face to the sun, feeling its benign warmth. For the first time in months she smiled, her sister's hand still clutched in hers.

Frogspawn and

Writer Valery McConnell and **Yours** *readers remember the highs, but mainly lows, of school dinners*

The slime, the smells, the gristle! Reading your memories of school dinners, I had a flashback - or should I say a 'smellback'. It was the really unpleasant odour of rancid cooking oil that my primary school's home-cooked crisps had been deep-fried in. The crisps themselves used to stick together in great greasy lumps and the thought of them now still makes me feel queasy.

While some of you did love school dinners and, like **Sue Rowley**, waxed lyrical about "roasts, complete with potatoes which were fluffy inside and crisp on the outside, tasty pies, fresh vegetables and salads followed by puddings - steamed and baked, always with custard, and my favourite - chocolate concrete, a sort of

shortbread flavoured with chocolate which was served with pink custard," she was in the minority. More, like me, recalled lumpy potatoes, shoe-leather meat and, my particular horror, butter beans cooked in scummy water that left them covered in sinister dark cracks.

Sue Buckey has her own bean horror story. "The worst experience I had was the day we had salad. I am convinced that all the leftovers were used from the previous day, as the lettuce was liberally sprinkled with cold peas, diced cold vegetables etc.

"Haricot beans were also included, but one day one of my beans was darker than the rest. I noticed this just as I was about to put it into my mouth so I rejected it and placed it carefully

on the side of my plate. A few minutes later it started to walk round my plate. It was a small slug."

But you fought back with the resourcefulness worthy of an escapee from Colditz. "I boarded in the week," emails **Jean Tripp**. "Every Thursday we were served macaroni cheese. Whether you liked it or not was no concern of the nuns. You ate it. I, however, felt physically sick whenever I saw the big pan on the trolley and after my plate was handed to me (and the nun wasn't looking) I would scoop it up and put it in my gymslip pocket! My mother was not amused when I arrived home on the Friday evening."

Great young minds think alike... "I loathed cabbage and sprouts," writes **Jean Ellacott**. "As luck would have it, school knickers in those days were thick, with a pocket for your hankie. My pocket was used for that horrible green vegetable. I often wonder what I smelt like for the afternoon lessons."

Sheila Milstead's chum was even more bold. "One girl had a discoloured potato on her plate. She put it on the end of her spoon and flicked it out of the open window. Her aim was spot on but it landed next to a girl from the gardening group who was weeding a flowerbed.

Unbelievably, she carried it back into the dining hall. Questions were asked and the

This was our village infants' school 72 years ago. Our dinners were served on our desks and afterwards we had a sleep.

Joan Risely, Cumbria

dead man's arm

In 1949 there was a special delivery of rice pudding to my grammar school in north London. As rationing was still in existence, photographs were taken of the event – so this is me enjoying it!

Peggy Pickering, Middx

culprit owned up, but was not forced to eat it. We had plenty to say to the so-called gardener."

I should think so - she needed to take lessons in solidarity from **Jenny Disley's** lovely friend... "I hated tapioca (frogspawn) with a passion," Jenny writes. "I knew I could never get it down and so refused. I was made to sit at the table until I ate it while a teacher watched me. I was there all lunchtime. Just before classes started again, my dear friend Caroline came over to me with her new expensive leather satchel (most of us only had

canvas ones). She gave me a hug and a grin and tipped my bowl of tapioca into her beautiful satchel. What an amazing friend."

Some of you got your revenge on lunchtime tyrants. **Allie Drewery**: "I absolutely hated mashed swede, so on this particular day when I was served it, I left it on the side. Upon seeing this a strict dinner lady insisted I would sit there until it was finished. I tried and tried and eventually, with her barking at me I tried to force it down and was promptly sick all over the floor."

Lena Walton's sister: "One day, one of my sister's classmates came running to me to tell me my sister had been forced to eat the revolting concoction we called worms - spaghetti bolognaise with cheese. Karen had, instead of complying with the order to eat it, thrown the plate of worms at the headmistress. I arrived at the scene of 'worm-gate' to see the headmistress march out of the unusually silent dinner hall covered in spaghetti. I have to admit even now, more than 40 years later, I have a secret respect for her behaviour." Me too!

By the way, in case you don't know, dead man's arm is rolypoly suet pudding filled with mince!

Hallo, handsome

Judith dreams of a holiday romance – but Jean disapproves!

Judith tried to ignore the fluttering in her stomach as she approached the bar. The barman gave her a warm smile and asked: "Same again?" His ocean-blue eyes gazed into hers as he awaited her response.

"Yes, please," she replied, returning the smile. She could feel Jean's glare burning holes into her back. In fact, Jean had spotted the dashing barman first. Judith tried to dismiss her guilt – after all Jean had a husband to go home to and she didn't. Rex had been dead five years now and she missed male company. It didn't seem like five years; she still rolled over some mornings and expected to find her sleeping husband beside her. She missed watching the rise and fall of his chest as he slept, and hearing the sound of his gentle breathing.

Ever since Rex had passed away Jean had made a point of accompanying her on an annual holiday. This year the destination had been the west coast of Ireland. Judith fell instantly in love with the rugged coastline and stony beaches. She found the bite of the sea breeze refreshing. Jean complained of the damp and the dreariness. "I knew we should have gone to Spain again!" she moaned. "This place is freezing!"

"There you go," the barman said, placing the drinks on the counter. Judith fumbled with her purse: "I just can't get used to this currency."

The barman laughed. "Here, let me help you." He leaned further over the counter. The smell of his aftershave made her tingle. He looked to be in his late 30s; his raven black hair peppered with grey. It reminded her of that actor that Jean cooed about when they'd been to the cinema the night before. Sometimes it amazed Judith that Jean's marriage had survived all these years – her gaze was always wandering.

She smiled secretly to herself as she remembered what Rex used to say whenever he noticed her admiring a stranger. Nudging her playfully, he'd whisper: "Lucky I'm not the jealous type."

Judith couldn't help being flirtatious. Her late husband had been no George Clooney. His attraction lay in his gentle nature and quick wit. She was glad that her new fancy, with his chiselled good looks, was so different. She didn't want a substitute. If she were ever to love another man she wanted to love them for different reasons. She doubted that anyone could ever reach her as her husband had done.

Her thoughts were once again interrupted by the man behind the bar. "That's the right amount," he said kindly, showing her the money he'd taken from her purse.

"I'll believe you – this time," she teased.

He pretended to be wounded. "I'm a honest man!" he protested merrily. She heard herself give a girlish giggle and once again she felt Jean's disapproving frown boring into her back.

She told herself she should be sensible – after all, he was a barman, he was paid to be friendly. Seeing his name badge, she couldn't resist asking: "How long have you been working here, Danny?"

He smiled pleasantly and she noticed that he had gorgeous dimples. His eyes twinkled roguishly: "Three seasons now. Seems like a life sentence."

Judith looked through the large window at the mighty Atlantic waves rolling into the bay, and said: "I can think of worse places to spend my time."

> **"If she were ever to love another man she wanted to love them for different reasons. She doubted anyone could ever reach her as her husband had done"**

His expression changed and she guessed that underneath his blarney he respected his beautiful surroundings. He nodded: "It's impressive all right."

She found her gaze straying toward his left hand, but there was no wedding band there. "Are you from around here?" she asked.

He nodded: "Born and bred."

She loved his Irish brogue and the way his eyes held her gaze.

"Where are ye from?" he enquired, tilting his head towards where Jean was sitting, waiting for her drink.

"London," she replied, feeling herself going pink at his interest.

"I have a sister living in London," he told her

WORDS: JENNIFER KISSANE/ILLUSTRATION: KATE DAVIES

and they continued to chat with ease until he enquired: "Is your husband with you?"

Judith felt a lump in her throat: "No. He passed away a few years ago."

Danny blushed furiously. "I'm so sorry," he stammered. "I saw your wedding ring and presumed..."

She regained her composure and felt glad that she had the ability to put the handsome man at ease. "Don't worry," she smiled reassuringly. He was clearly still embarrassed so she continued: "Are you in a relationship?"

His confidence restored, he shook his head and laughed: "No. Who would have me?"

Judith's stomach did a somersault and she felt goose bumps on her arms. She looked quickly over her shoulder to see Jean striding toward them with a face like thunder. Why couldn't Jean accept that she was just having a bit of fun? Since Rex had died Judith missed being a woman who revelled in male attention. Her husband had always been an old-fashioned romantic, knowing when to shower her with compliments and kisses.

Maybe chatting up the barman had been a bit out of character, but she had just felt the need to enjoy some masculine flattery...

Jean grabbed the drinks and pulled her firmly away from the bar, saying: "For goodness' sake, Mother, remember you'll be 75 next birthday!"

Two-speed crossword

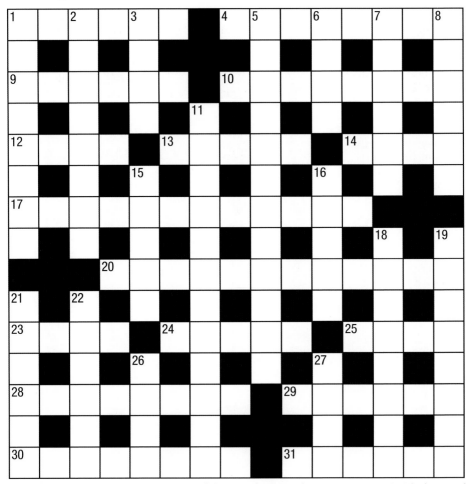

For this puzzle we've provided two sets of clues, each giving the same answers. Quick clues are below and Cryptic to the right. It's a good way to hone your skills, because it gives you two ways to crack the crossword!

ACROSS
1 Murray - - -, retired sports commentator (6)
4 Calculate roughly (8)
9 Bounty, prize (6)
10 Mount - - -, volcano that erupted in 1980 (2, 6)
12 Overwhelming defeat (4)
13 Passenger vessel (5)
14 Periphery (4)
17 Biro (9, 3)
20 Tennis format in which men and women play together (5, 7)
23 Askew (4)
24 Raw vegetable dish (5)
25 Domed recess in a place of worship (4)
28 Boney M song (8)
29 Macaw or cockatoo? (6)
30 Treat as irrelevant (8)
31 University buildings and surrounding estate (6)

DOWN
1 Cupboard for clothes (8)
2 Legally (8)
3 Continental currency (4)
5 Common constituent of unhealthy food (9, 3)
6 Brainwave (4)
7 Meeting's order of business (6)
8 Christian festival (6)
11 Serious thought (12)
15 Iberian country (5)
16 Venue of the 1988 Summer Olympics (5)
18 Foolish talk (8)
19 Banned building material (8)
21 Extreme dislike (6)
22 Catastrophe (6)
26 Japanese combat sport practised at a basho (4)
27 Word representing P in the phonetic alphabet (4)

ACROSS

1 Pedestrian initially leapt into boat's trail on river (6)
4 Guess teatime's rearranged (8)
9 Draughtsman returned for recompense (6)
10 Street's housing beautiful woman in Merseyside town (2, 6)
12 Hiding right away from home (4)
13 Transport Bryan the singer (5)
14 Acknowledges holding advantage (4)
17 Item of stationery – function: to indicate enclosure (9, 3)
20 At Wimbledon, some pairs served large gin and tonics? (5, 7)
23 Answer: drily humorous with a twist (4)
24 Daughter unfortunately returned side dish (5)
25 Afterthought following article on Eastern section of church (4)
28 'Mad Monk' baffled puritans (8)
29 Bird evolved from raptor (6)
30 Senior detectives calculate reduction in price (8)
31 College grounds: this is where tents are pitched by you and me (6)

DOWN

1 Fighting doctor over award for furniture (8)
2 In accordance with regulations, left in a dreadful way (8)
3 Neurotic concealing money in Ireland, eg (4)
5 Roman god mostly consumed terribly daft stuff found in dairy (9, 3)
6 I would forget half of each thought (4)
7 Underlying motive from a male or female, reportedly (6)
8 Diner receives second spring holiday (6)
11 Debate how the French write of emancipation (12)
15 End of needless suffering for European nation (5)
16 South Korean city with single on the radio? (5)
18 Applaud means of catching rubbish (8)
19 Muddled boss eats dangerous substance (8)
21 Loathing crimson headgear at first (6)
22 Credit is double trouble (6)
26 Numerical problem with ring for wrestling (4)
27 Two personal assistants for dad (4)

Wordsearch 2

Can you find all these British Prime Ministers?

ADDINGTON	JENKINSON
ASQUITH	MACMILLAN
ATTLEE	MAJOR
BALDWIN	NORTH
BLAIR	PITT
CALLAGHAN	STANLEY
CAMERON	THATCHER
CHURCHILL	WALPOLE
DISRAELI	WELLESLEY
GLADSTONE	WILSON

```
D Z Z O K T T I P M
H T R O N W R V Q A A
A P K S P I H W C M D
T X L W A L T M Q Q D
T D Z L Y X I N J W I
L H B T E L U O F B N
E H N H L C Q S D J G
E D S A S A S N A M T
G I N T E L A I U A O
L S P C L L W K I J N
A R U H L A I N Y O Q
D A W E E G L E O R T
S E A R W H S J U B T
T L L F J A O R N U L
O I P D I N N H I G D
N O O B A L D W I N I
E J L U D L L C V F M
V Y E L N A T S S C V
L L I H C R U H C Z B
C A M E R O N Z J F L
```

Were you right? Turn to page 182 for the answers

Hat's off to

All her life, Rose has failed to look good in a hat...

Maureen said: "I must say you are making an effort." She didn't actually add 'for once' but Rose, standing in front of the mirror, sensed the unspoken comment. She hardly recognised herself; the blue dress and jacket looked strange – casual shirts and trousers were more her line.

"Aren't you going to do something with your hair?" Maureen asked.

"In a minute." Rose tried not to snap. She rifled through her bag for a comb, then tipped the contents on to the bed. Lipsticks, tissues and a mascara rolled across the quilt. She heard Maureen's indrawn breath as she attacked her mane of blonde hair. The comb had two teeth missing – Maureen was sure to notice that.

"I don't believe it!" Maureen was peering into the carrier bag beside the dressing table. "You've got a hat! Whatever possessed you?"

Rose didn't know what had possessed her. She'd never liked hats. Her earliest memory was of her mother putting a sun hat on her at the seaside. There she'd been, pretending to be a mermaid singing on a rock, when two hands descended out of nowhere and she felt she'd been snuffed out like a candle. Rose still recalled her deep sense of affront that anyone should cover her golden curls.

School was the worst. In those far-off days girls' uniforms included hats. Nasty felt hats, shaped like pudding basins with scratchy elastic under the chin.

"Rose Burton, where is your hat?" was the question forever on the lips of any member of staff who spotted her coming through the gates, bareheaded. Sometimes the hat was squashed in her satchel, sometimes hanging carelessly down her back.

"Young ladies attending St Hilary's wear hats in the street," the headmistress informed her sternly. Detention made no difference and neither did exclusion from hockey. Rose hadn't cared. She preferred to read or paint.

"Really, darling," her mother said sadly after the third letter from the school, "Maureen always gets good conduct marks, I do think you might make an effort."

"But I DO work!" Rose protested. And she did.

There was never any complaint about the effort she put in to lessons – only about her appearance.

"Hats are stupid," she declared, "and the school hat makes me look hideous. Anyway, wearing a hat won't make any difference when I leave school."

Her mother sighed again. "Well, darling, just try, will you? To please me."

Martyr-like, Rose set off the following morning. It was summer so she wore a straw boater with a blue-and-green band – fastened with the inevitable elastic. The day was hot. Rose loosened the hat. A draught from a passing van caught it, and sucked it under the wheels. The tyre marks made an interesting pattern but it was too squashed to wear.

> **"The wedding photographs were charming, except that Rose's wide-brimmed lilac hat had somehow fallen off and been sat on by a guest"**

When Rose was in the sixth form, she went on a school trip to France. The girls all wore attractive new berets but 20 minutes out of Dover and Rose's fell into the Channel as she leaned over the rail to look at the white cliffs.

"Oh, Rose!" exclaimed her mother in despair when she heard the tale. Despair turned to desperation when Rose was Maureen's bridesmaid. The wedding photographs were charming, except that Rose's wide-brimmed lilac hat had somehow fallen off and been sat on by a guest.

"I can't help my hair," Rose had once said to her mother. By then she was a rising star in the field of interior design with her own casual style of dress. "I suppose you'd rather I kept my crowning glory hidden. Anyway, what is it about hats?"

"I just think they finish off an outfit," her mother who was in her 60s and still wore a hat although they were no longer fashionable, explained. "Maureen always manages to look

WORDS: ANGELA LANYON/ILLUSTRATION: KATE DAVIES

Mother

smart even with three children to look after."

Rose tried not to sound resentful when she replied. "Maureen's always done the right thing, hasn't she?" I suppose you'd think more of me if I wore a hat and had a proper marriage licence instead of living with Tom."

Rose was successful enough to buy any number of expensive outfits and smart hats but when she spent so much time going up and down ladders and clambering about partly refurbished houses there wasn't much point. When she did wear a hat it was a safety helmet.

That conversation had been just a fortnight ago, the last time she had seen her mother. She had taken Rose's hand and laughed: "I love you just the same, with or without a hat."

Rose wondered now if she'd meant it.

She smoothed her skirt and her sister's eyes met hers in the mirror. Maureen passed her the carrier bag and Rose took out the hat. It was blue with blue-and-green ribbons, rather like the band on her school hat. Blue for the sky and green for the grass...

The hat had a wide brim and two feathers on one side. Instead of elastic to keep it in place, there was an elegant hatpin. She skewered it carefully through her hair. This time the hat was going to stay put.

Tom squeezed her fingers as they stood by the graveside. The coffin seemed small and lonely as it was lowered into the earth. It was a calm summer's day, then from nowhere came a gust of wind, lifting Rose's hat and spinning it over the wall. As she watched it disappear, Rose was sure she heard her mother's ghostly laugh.

Thrown in at

*Writer Valery McConnell and **Yours** readers remember the pleasures and terrors of learning to swim...*

PIC: ALAMY STOCK PHOTO

When I was a child, it seemed that swimming pools and verrucas went together like The Lone Ranger and Tonto. So although my primary school actually had an outdoor pool, I spent most of the summer term glumly sitting on the side, infectious foot stuck inside its plimsoll, while my lucky classmates frolicked in the water. I managed my ten yards certificate in a splashy doggy paddle, but never learned anything more elegant. However I don't remember being taught with anything but kindness or any teacher wielding an implement that features strongly in many of your anecdotes - the dreaded hooked pole!

Mary Sharp's is typical: "When I was 12 years old, our teacher took us swimming. I was very scared and stayed in behind the shallow end until a schoolfriend came up behind me and tossed me over the top into the deep end. I floundered and

went down. Then the lifeguard, using a long pole, caught me and hauled me out by my drawers. To this day I still remember how embarrassed I felt in front of all the other children laughing their heads off."

Patricia Mayne could only face it down as an adult... "I was pushed into the deep end in a swimming pool when young and consequently lost all confidence. When I was 38 I decided to have lessons and finding ladies in their 80s at the class made me think, 'If they can do it, so can I'. To get our certificate, we had to swim a length of the pool while the instructor walked along beside us holding a long pole with a hook on the end. I'm sure it's what made me keep going because there was no way I was going to be pulled out of the water on the end of a hook!"

No reminiscences would be complete without a knitted cossie story... "When I was 12 I went to a new school where we had swimming lessons," writes **Margaret Whittle**.

"Money was short so my mother knitted me a swimsuit. It was bright yellow with black stripes. I looked like a wasp. When it was wet, it stretched down past my knees and the wool weighed a ton. No wonder I never learned to swim." And a million over-60s nod in sympathy.

My friend Valerie and I at the swimming pool at Uxbridge (above). It didn't take us long to get out of the paddling pool.
Barbara Bignell, Northants

But some of you were going to sink, whatever you were wearing. Like **Marion Hobbins**... "My teacher, Miss Phillips, would tie her coat belt to the straps of my costume and make me do the actions while she walked along the top holding me up. Then she would let go and I would unceremoniously sink like a submarine. I still cannot swim."

Linda Spooner's desperate teacher tried, "armbands, a rubber ring and a rope all at the same time with her pulling me along. But I was just relieved when the lesson ended - and cannot swim to this day."

Swimming-refusenik **Brenda Martin** had it sussed from the word go. "Aged 13, we had to walk in a crocodile to the nearest baths and I hated the thought of swimming. On the second week I had a period, so

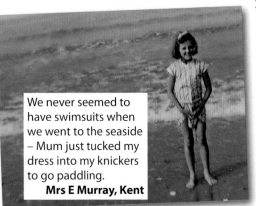

We never seemed to have swimsuits when we went to the seaside – Mum just tucked my dress into my knickers to go paddling.
Mrs E Murray, Kent

the deep end

my mother gave me a note to be excused, which the instructor gave back to me. So every couple of weeks when we went to the baths I produced this note. It worked because the instructor was always a different person."

She was probably wise as so many of you were put off swimming for life by cruel instructors. **Monica Colley** remembers, "The instructor lined us nine-year-olds up at the deep end of the open-air unheated pool. He then walked along the back of everyone and pushed them in. Not only was this a shock, the water was freezing and I didn't stop shaking all day."

Sheila Wilde was being taught at the local baths, aged 11. "We were all lined up in the pool holding onto the edge and the female instructor told us to put our heads under the water.

Some of us were frightened so she pushed our heads down. My dad, who worked nightshifts and had come along to watch, blasted the instructor for her actions but the damage was done. I never went back. "

And even if they were not physical bullies, it seems swimming instructors just weren't programmed to make us feel good about ourselves, as **Nora Ridley** discovered. "In my 30s I decided it was time to conquer my fears and learn to swim, so I enrolled in adult classes. The instructor did not look kindly on a 30-something adult clinging to the side of the pool. From her lofty position she looked down and asked, 'Have you ever cooked mince?' 'Yes,' came my mystified reply. 'What happens to the fat when the mince goes cold?' 'It floats to the

Me in my knitted swimsuit – not to mention cardi, socks and sandals – on holiday at Butlins.
Mrs M Mynett, Oldham

top.' 'Then dear,' she proclaimed, 'why are you afraid of the water? You are not going to drown.' That was my first and last swimming lesson at that pool. I eventually did teach myself to swim."

Life in the

Amy finds learning to drive with Dad is a bumpy ride!

WORDS: BEATRICE CHARLES/ILLUSTRATION: CLAIRE FLETCHER

Joan asked: "How are you enjoying your driving lessons, Amy?"

"Oh, don't ask," her granddaughter moaned, flopping down on the sofa beside her. "Dad is so impatient! I crunched the gears today and you should have heard him going on. All he does is criticise. You would think he was the perfect driver."

"Perfect?" chuckled Joan. "I could tell you some tales about your dad."

Oh, do, Gran. Please!" Amy relaxed and snuggled up; Joan was a good storyteller.

"Well, I ought to start when he was five years old. Your dad had been given a three-wheeler bike for his birthday and he thought he was Evel Knievel! He managed to get four boys on the tricycle with him, they took a corner too fast and they all fell off."

"Were they hurt?"

"The others were alright, just a few cuts and bruises, but your dad ended up with both arms in plaster. I had to wash and feed him like a baby. And his poor bike never recovered. Granddad managed to fix it but it always made a funny clunking noise after that.

"Then there was the go-kart he made himself from an old set of pram wheels, a wooden plank and a length of rope to steer it. It had one major design fault - no brakes! You can guess what happened."

"Did he crash?" asked Amy, trying not to laugh.

"He hit a lamppost, broke his front tooth and was limping for days. Then there was the motorbike..."

"A motorbike? My dad on a motorbike?" Amy interrupted, amazed at the thought of her oh-so-serious father being such a daredevil.

"Well, it was really a motor scooter. He was just 16 and so proud of it. Saved up for it from his wages and bought it from a friend who had joined the army. He spent every spare hour in the back yard tinkering with it. I lost count of the number of shirts he got covered in oil before he bought some proper overalls."

"Then there was the motorbike..."
"A motorbike? My dad on a motorbike?"
Amy interrupted, amazed at the thought
of her oh-so-serious father being
such a daredevil

"But what happened?" prompted Amy.

"Well, he was late for work one day and tried to take a shortcut across a field. He skidded in the mud and landed up to his waist in a drainage ditch. The farmer had been spreading slurry the day before so when he wheeled the scooter home he had a trail of flies after him. What a stink! I refused to

let him in the house until he had stripped off his dirty clothes. Your granddad had to hose him down in the yard."

Amy giggled delightedly at the image of her father dripping wet in his underclothes.

Joan continued: "He never lived that down. The lads at the factory used to tease him for weeks afterwards, holding their noses and swatting imaginary flies away! Anyway, after that episode he started to save for some proper driving lessons. We didn't have a car ourselves so he had to practise with Uncle Harold in his old Ford.

"Poor Uncle Harold! I don't think he knew what he was letting himself in for. He said your dad would never pass his test as he was too hotheaded. As it was, it took him seven attempts before he finally succeeded."

"Seven?" Amy asked incredulously.

"Yes, seven. But do you know what finally turned your dad into a careful driver?"

Amy shook her head.

"It was when you were born and he drove you and your

fast lane

test. And when you do, I want you to give me some lessons."

"Driving lessons?" Amy looked surprised. "I won't be allowed to teach anyone to drive for years, Gran."

"No, not driving as such. The thing is," Joan confided, "I've ordered a mobility scooter and I'm feeling a little nervous about using it. There's no way I'd ask your dad to teach me – he'd have me doing wheelies! No, what I need is a sensible, careful driver to help me with the rules of the road, understanding traffic signs, all that sort of thing."

"Of course, Gran. I'd be glad to help. In fact, perhaps you can begin by testing me on the Highway Code ready for my theory test."

"What a good idea. That way we can learn together," Joan said with a smile.

Later that evening Joan phoned her son, Robert, to tell him that she thought their plan had worked. He had been worried that Amy wasn't taking her driving lessons seriously enough and that she drove too impetuously.

He sounded relieved and said: "Thanks, Mum. I was beginning to think my daughter was in danger of taking life in the fast lane a bit too literally!"

When she hung up, Joan smiled wryly to herself, knowing only too well who it was that Amy took after.

mum home from the hospital. He grew up overnight and all the bravado of youth went. No more speeding or fast cornering. He drove very carefully with his precious family in the car.

"So if your dad is impatient with you, remember it's because he wants to keep you

safe. One day soon you will be independent and he won't be there to protect you. That's a hard thing for any parent."

"Thanks, Gran. That does help me to understand."

"You'll be a good driver, Amy, and I'm sure it won't take you seven attempts to pass your

Two-speed crossword

For this puzzle we've provided two sets of clues, each giving the same answers. Quick clues are below and Cryptic to the right. It's a good way to hone your skills, because it gives you two ways to crack the crossword!

ACROSS
1   Scribble (6)
5   One-way ticket (6)
10 Grooming aid (9)
11 Chef's tall white hat (5)
12 Footwear for muddy conditions (10, 5)
13 Hand in one's notice (6)
15 Strictness (8)
17 Catholic supplication (4, 4)
19 Orb (6)
23 Movie starring Humphrey Bogart and Katharine Hepburn (3, 7, 5)
25 Model of ethical behaviour (5)
26 - - - Day, Christian festival celebrated on 1 November (3, 6)
27 Fish-eating bird (6)
28 List or describe completely (6)

DOWN
2   Feverish cold (5)
3   Walking in a leisurely manner (7)
4   Living room (6)
5   Speedy sailing ship (8)
6   Important (7)
7   Plant root used to make confectionery (9)
8   Brief spell of rain (6)
9   Mean, scant (6)
14 Cowardly (9)
16 Regular, plain (8)
17 - - - balloon, means of transport (3,3)
18 Car's silencer (7)
20 Agreeably tart (7)
21 - - - Shackleton, Antarctic explorer (6)
22 Slow and sentimental song (6)
24 Feeling of agitated dissatisfaction (5)

ACROSS

1 Advance slowly after head of school produces messy handwriting (6)
5 Solitary record (6)
10 Bristly lock keeper? (9)
11 Incorrectly quote something off the top of your head, perhaps (5)
12 Capital trunks! Essential wear for splashing about? (10, 5)
13 Quit period of rule (with small interruption) (6)
15 Austerity: cut it by start of year (8)
17 Prayer had mostly transformed my lair (4, 4)
19 Globe showing southern power in this place (6)
23 Classic adventure movie like Cleopatra? (3, 7, 5)
25 One bargain is perfect (5)
26 Pop group who are totally angelic? (3, 6)
27 Carnivorous bird turned so on victim (6)
28 Particular aspect of French aircraft's back end (6)

DOWN

2 Church beneath which I'll relax (5)
3 Casually going and making bets, but losing head (7)
4 Room to pounce around ring (6)
5 Large glass vessel (8)
6 Striking absence of dining room furniture? (7)
7 Sweet alcoholic drink with something cooling (9)
8 Display the Queen's washing cubicle! (6)
9 Pitiful to be suffering from rubella? (6)
14 Frightened like an invertebrate (9)
16 Unexceptional wrought iron yard (8)
17 Trendy to broadcast empty talk (3, 3)
18 Two females split backless shoe and royal scarf (7)
20 Sharp quip rewritten by worker (7)
21 'Cockney girl's home,' announced Mr Hemingway (6)
22 Commercial follows dance song (6)
24 Boredom is a hidden nuisance, somewhat (5)

Wordsearch 3

Can you find all the words associated with being creative?

ACCOMPLISH	FABRICATE
ACHIEVE	FORMULATE
ARTISTIC	INSPIRATION
ASSEMBLE	INTUITIVE
CONCOCT	ORIGINAL
CONSTRUCT	PROCESS
CONTRIVE	TALENTED
CULTIVATE	VISIONARY
DEVISE	

```
H O H C R P T E G E V
I D K O E R A T T A D
A E D N V O L A V B B
G V F C I C E C M A N
T I S O R E N I C N A
F S M C T S T R L B C
N E E T N S E B A E H
U O V H O I D A C T I
I E I V C T G F C A E
E T T X I D D O V V
C A I E A Y R D M I E
C L U L E R K P P T X
O U T B A A I M L L F
N M N M U N J P I U V
S R I E X O I X S C C
T O V S E I Z G H N L
R F X S V S M J I F I
U I F A E I V Y M R I
C V M F G V C H J C O
T A R T I S T I C P W
```

Were you right? Turn to page 182 for the answers

Rags to riches

Cissie's little dog leads her a merry dance...

Cissie Markham glanced at the calendar. May 23, 1968. Her 44th birthday. Where had the time gone?

She watched a group of teenage girls in mini skirts stroll past her window. Her teenage years had borne no comparison to theirs – the war had seen to that. She'd met and married Jim in 1943 when she was 19. Their happiness was brief as he was killed in action the following year.

Since then she'd dedicated her life to nursing, but she had her memories. She smiled as she saw a young couple walking hand in hand. The boy was serenading his girl with the Beatles' song, From Me to You. Not quite the same as We'll Meet Again, Cissie reflected wryly.

Giving herself a shake, she said briskly: "Come on, Rags, time for your walk. I think we'll go along by the canal." The mongrel wagged his tail and sat while she clipped on his lead.

There was only one boat moored on the canal, its red and green livery shining in the spring sunlight. Cissie recognised the name, The Lady Elizabeth. It had been moored in the same place last year.

At that moment, she stumbled on the uneven towpath and Rags seized the chance to slip his lead and dash towards the narrow boat. "Come back, you rascal!"

Too late. The dog had jumped aboard, wagging his tail furiously at the man who opened the door to see what was happening.

"I'm so sorry – he slipped his lead."

The man beamed. "That's all right. We don't mind, do we, boy?" He bent down and patted Rags on the head. "In fact, I believe I have something for you." Reaching inside, he produced a doggie chew and Rags became even more excited at this unexpected treat.

"That's very kind of you, Mr – "

"Oh, call me Bill, please," he smiled, stroking his bushy white beard. "And you are?"

"Cissie – Cissie Markham. And this little scoundrel is Rags."

Rags cocked his head to one side and Bill laughed: "Your mistress is right – you are a little scoundrel!"

Cissie felt surprisingly at ease with the stranger with the twinkling blue eyes. Sporting a Breton cap and striped jersey, he looked a typical sailor. She guessed him to be in his 50s; his weatherbeaten face testament to an outdoor life.

He said: "I remember you and Rags passing by my window the last time I was this way."

"I remember your boat, but not you," Cissie replied, then blushed. "I'm sorry, that sounds quite rude."

Bill laughed: "No at all!" He raised his cap and ran his fingers though his shock of white hair. "Would you think it forward of me if I invited you in for a cup of tea?"

Before she could reply, Rags bounded through the open door. She smiled: "Seems like Rags has made the decision for me."

Cissie gasped in surprise at the boat's neat interior with its shiny black-leaded range and beautiful ribbon plates on the walls. "This is beautiful, Bill. I had no idea! Do you live on board?"

He nodded. "It's something I've always wanted to do so when I took early retirement I bought The Lady Elizabeth."

The kettle on the range began to whistle and soon they were drinking tea while Rags played with an old toy that Bill told her used to belong to his dog, Buster. "I lost him a few months back. A finer friend a man never had."

He sat quietly, deep in thought, before saying:

"Cissie felt surprisingly at ease with the stranger with the twinkling blue eyes... he looked a typical sailor"

"Life can be lonely, don't you find, Cissie? I lost my Elizabeth in the Blitz and there has never been anyone to take her place."

Cissie murmured sympathetically and Bill said: "I presume that you, too, are on your own?" Blushing, he immediately apologised: "Please forgive me – that was too outspoken by far. I'm sorry."

WORDS: MARION FELLOWS/ILLUSTRATION: KATE DAVIES

"There's no need to apologise. You are right, I am on my own. As it happens, I also lost my Jim in the war. His ship, The Serendipity, was torpedoed."

The colour drained from Bill's face. "You mean your husband served on The Serendipity?"

Cissie nodded.

Bill clasped her hands in his. "I was on that ship, Cissie!"

As if dazed, he got to his feet, went over to the sideboard and picked up a framed photograph. "I knew your husband. I knew Jim Markham." Looking at the picture, he went on: "In fact, we shared a cabin; we were buddies. He was a grand fellow."

He handed the photo to Cissie and her eyes met those of the smiling, handsome sailor standing at the back of the group. A single tear fell on the glass. She looked up: "Then you must be Bill Baxter."

"Well, I'll be blowed." He shook his head in disbelief. "Cissie Markham. Jim told me so much about you, I feel I know you already." Taking her hand, he said with a catch in his voice: "I think Jim would be pleased to know we'd found each other."

Cissie looked once more at the photo and then at Bill and responded to the affectionate squeeze of his hand. "So do I, Bill."

Then they laughed as Rags jumped up and excitedly tried to lick them both at once.

'Press button A'

Writer, Valery McConnell and **Yours** *readers remember when the only phone was at the end of the street...*

Clever go-between Rex carried love notes in his collar!

How do you make your grandchildren incredulous? Tell them that when you were young, there were no mobile phones and many of us didn't even have a landline.

As a student in digs in the mid-Seventies, the phone box at the end of our street didn't have any glass, so in the winter you would have to wipe the snow off the dial before trying to get through. But at least my mum always appreciated my call...

"In the winter of 1974," emails **Diane Kell**, "My army husband was on a tour in Belfast. We lived in military quarters and didn't have a phone, so every evening the wives would gather at the only telephone box.

"One evening, my husband spoke to me quite grumpily when I got through, complaining I'd rung while Top of the Pops was on and he missed the No. 1 single. Never mind I'd been standing freezing in the cold to

check he was OK!"

Go back a decade and those Forces' phone calls required even more military precision. "In 1960," recalls **A B Paice**, "I was a boy soldier stationed in Harrogate and my girlfriend was living in Wrexham. To speak to her, I had to first write and ask her to be near a specific phone box at a certain time. Then I would walk two miles to a phone, hope it wasn't busy and ask the operator for a 'person to person' call to make sure I was actually going to speak to my girlfriend. This cost extra. Once the operator had established that it was my girlfriend, I was then requested to push button A to connect. My allocated three minutes started counting down until we were cut off."

But planning could have its charms... "When I met my husband-to-be on holiday, I lived in Lancashire and he lived in Cheshire," writes **Marjorie Roberts**. "We didn't have a home phone so I used to walk to a phone box at an arranged time for him to call me. After chatting we would then arrange a time to both play our records simultaneously and think of each other. We married 12 months later."

John Nicholls' story has a musical theme too: "Nearly 60 years ago, we teenagers were allowed limited use of our Dansette record players as our parents didn't appreciate rock 'n'

roll - or the constant need to put money in the meter. One of our gang realised that by changing the plug on her record player and using the light socket in the street phone box, we could enjoy free music! Happy Days!"

But phones weren't just about fun. "In the Sixties we had no house phone," emails **Rose Janes**. "I had been on a school trip and when dropped at the nearest town, realised I had missed the last bus home! I knew my mother would be waiting at the nearest bus stop to our home - three miles away. I was tired and very frightened but found a phone box and rang a neighbouring farm. The farmer went to my home, told my dad where I was, then he drove his car to the bus stop to tell my mum and she drove to town to collect me. What a performance!"

Pat Berkshire's mum might have been glad of a phone, too. "My dad was in the merchant navy and my parents communicated by letter, telegram and telephone

Ann Rowe and workmate Pat in 1968. Their office phone was used to conduct romances!

PIC: GETTY IMAGES

message from Dad via the village post office. One message read: "Arriving Immingham docks Friday, sailing Tuesday. Join me for weekend. Bring hat." I was very indignant to be packed off to my grandparents and Mum couldn't understand why Dad wanted his hat. On meeting Mum, Dad's first words were, "Where's Pat?" The message should have read, "Bring Pat"!

The important thing is that the message gets through, as **Glennys Wood** knew: "In 1961, I was diagnosed with appendicitis and the doctor ordered me an ambulance. I had to let my boyfriend know what was happening, so walked to the nearest phone box. While there, I fainted, came round, passed on the message and walked back to meet the ambulance!"

Who needs a phone when you've got a pet?. "My dog Rex would often come with me to my boyfriend's house," writes **Mrs Roper**. "One day he came home with a note tucked in his collar. He had gone round to the house himself. It was a great way to stay in touch. After we married, Rex would still go to visit and got a biscuit in a paper bag to take home!"

The boy next door

Arthur finds that age is no barrier to friendship

A voice asked: "What are you doing?"

From his ladder, Arthur looked round to locate who had spoken. Standing in the next-door garden was a boy of around four with curly hair and blue eyes. "I'm cleaning the gutters."

"Why?"

"Because they get clogged up with leaves," explained Arthur.

"Are you Bob the Builder?"

"No, but I do fix things."

"Tom, leave the gentleman alone. He's busy." The boy's mother came into the garden. "I hope Tom's not bothering you. He's such a chatterbox."

"No bother at all. We were having a nice chat, weren't we, Tom? My name's Arthur, by the way."

"I'm Anna," she smiled up at him. "We'll see you around, Arthur. And do be careful up that ladder."

After they had gone inside, Arthur's thoughts turned to his grandchildren far away in Australia. He spoke to them on the phone every week and his daughter kept asking him to visit, but Arthur made excuses. It wouldn't be the same going without Lily.

A few days later he was digging the vegetable patch when he became aware of being watched through the slatted fence. "Hello, Tom!" he said cheerfully.

"What are you doing?"

"I'm planting some vegetables. Do you like vegetables?"

Tom pulled a face and Arthur laughed.

"Oh, you'll like my veg. Fresh from the garden. Wait there, Tom, I'm going to ask your mummy something."

Arthur knocked on the front door and Anna answered, looking frazzled. "Is it Tom? I hope he hasn't been bothering you. I sent him out to play while I decorate his bedroom."

"Not at all. What I came

"After they had gone inside, Arthur's thoughts turned to his grandchildren far away in Australia. His daughter kept asking him to visit, but Arthur made excuses"

---

to say was, would you like to join me for lunch? I've made pumpkin soup."

And so their friendship began.

Young Tom spent happy times with Arthur who taught him which seeds to plant, when to weed and how to turn the soil. In return, Arthur became a regular guest for Sunday lunch next door, providing vegetables from his garden.

If Anna needed any DIY jobs done, Arthur was always willing to help, with Tom as his trusty assistant.

The years passed. Arthur watched as Tom grew tall, his unruly curls gelled into place. The offers of help in the garden stopped as Tom spent more time with his teenage friends. Arthur missed his company, and he wasn't the only one.

"Sometimes I feel I don't know my own son any more," Anna sat at Tom's kitchen table helping him to slice runner beans.

"All teenagers go through that stage," Arthur tried to reassure her.

Anna sighed. "He never tells me where he's been or what he's been up to. When he's not out with his friends, he's holed up in his bedroom."

"Give him time. In the end he will come to realise that his best friend is his mum," Arthur advised, hoping that he was right.

Their conversation was still running through his mind when later that week he strolled through the park to the bowling club. He had volunteered to mend a broken lock on the clubhouse door but when he arrived he was surprised to find the door was ajar even though nobody was playing that afternoon.

Pushing it further open, Arthur called out, but there was no reply. He flicked the light

WORDS: BEATRICE CHARLES/ILLUSTRATION: CLAIRE FLETCHER

speaking as nausea overcame him.

"Oh, thank goodness! I thought you were..." Tom took a deep breath. "Lie still, Mr Davis. The ambulance is on its way."

While they waited, Tom explained that he had noticed the clubhouse door was open on his way home from school and had gone in to investigate.

When he visited Arthur in hospital the next day, the boy was more talkative than he had been for a long while. He said: "You are not to worry about a thing. I've watered your tomatoes and fed the cat. I'll put the bins out tomorrow morning."

"So it's you who is fixing things for me now, eh?"

"Well, it's what you've taught me to do," Tom replied with a shy smile. "You've always been a good neighbour to Mum and me."

Arthur said: "Your mum should be proud of you."

"Well, your accident made me realise how suddenly life can change. Mum and I have agreed we're going to spend more time together and from now on I'm going to join you in the garden every Saturday. I've missed helping you."

Tom's reaction made Arthur think hard about his own family. Six months later he walked through the arrivals gate at Sydney airport to be greeted with squeals of delight. "Dad! I'm so glad you're here at last. Tell me, what changed your mind?"

"Something a special young man said to me about life changing fast. I realised my grandchildren are growing up before I've spent precious time with them - so come on, let's go, I've lots of hugs to catch up on."

switch but it didn't work. The bulb probably needed changing. When he entered the cloakroom he was dismayed to find that intruders had left the taps on and the floor was flooded.

As he walked over to turn the water off, his foot slipped and he fell heavily, his head hitting the tiled floor. Everything went black.

Arthur woke to find someone leaning over him. As the figure came into focus, he realised it was a teenage boy, his face blotchy with tears.

"Tom!" He instantly regretted

Two-speed crossword

For this puzzle we've provided two sets of clues, each giving the same answers. Quick clues are below and Cryptic to the right. It's a good way to hone your skills, because it gives you two ways to crack the crossword!

ACROSS
3 Annie Lennox's band (10)
8 The - - -, no 1 song for Duran Duran in 1984 (6)
9 Relating to the Milky Way, eg (8)
10 Balderdash (8)
11 Catastrophic situation (6)
12 Regal (8)
15 Woman who works in a pub (7)
17 Outrageous topic of gossip (7)
19 Most deafening (8)
21 Warm and humid (6)
25 Waters between the UK and Scandinavia (5, 3)
26 Three goals from one player (3, 5)
27 Murray - - -, retired BBC sports commentator (6)
28 Potentially happening (2, 3, 5)

DOWN
1 Deviation from the expected path (6)
2 Ascends (6)
3 Demonstrative (10)
4 Scott Joplin's genre of music (7)
5 Plough, cultivate (4)
6 Native American shoe (8)
7 Spicy food flavouring (6)
11 Living quarters on a ship (5)
13 Traditional game also known as pick-up sticks (10)
14 White fish similar to cod (5)
16 Ill-suited pairing (8)
18 Very difficult puzzle (7)
20 Come into possession of (6)
22 Take a breath (6)
23 Zoo employee (6)
24 Flat circular object (4)

Puzzles

ACROSS

3 Pop duo of the 1980s try music he arranged (10)
8 Involuntary response regarding cable (6)
9 Cosmic lass right out of the frozen north (8)
10 Mr Hilfiger to perish? Nonsense! (8)
11 Credit is doubled for period of real trouble (6)
12 Grand joke with one caught following mum (8)
15 Prohibit male assistance for female serving drinks (7)
17 It's a disgrace to scrutinise lad coming back (7)
19 Loudest one taken in by most inquisitive (8)
21 Awkward adhesive (6)
25 The sonar is wrong where many oil rigs are found (5, 3)
26 Sporting feat is what you want from a magician and his rabbit? (3, 5)
27 Pedestrian comic named Roy (6)
28 Where birthday greetings may be likely? (2, 3, 5)

DOWN

1 Alternative route, end of road, then alternative route (6)
2 Increases talk of poetic regions (6)
3 Old newspapers I have are revealing (10)
4 Timothy, consumed by anger, makes notes on the piano? (7)
5 Store of cash hidden in Bastille (4)
6 Snake organised coin scam (8)
7 Hot food? One is after cold (6)
11 Hut initially contains a wastepaper basket (5)
13 Former Labour MP's entertainment for kids (10)
14 Mr Porter sits on tail of mighty fish (5)
16 Bond's boss is game for uneven contest (8)
18 Second fiddle is something funky! (7)
20 Acquire no bait in an unusual way (6)
22 Get a lungful in wintry weather, we're told (6)
23 Footballer to look up with hesitation (6)
24 Some undisclosed record (4)

Wordsearch 4

Can you find all these words which are connected to feeling good?

BLITHE	ENCHANT
CHEER	ENTHRAL
COMFORT	EXHILARATED
CONTENT	EXUBERANT
CONVIVIAL	GRATIFIED
DELIGHT	HAPPY
EBULLIENT	JOYOUS
ECSTASY	LAUGHTER
ELATION	OVERJOYED

```
G D E J V R O N E U T
I L E X B B N R X N C
J H E Y H L C B A F O
D Y X X O R I H E Q N
U B U K T J C T O K V
I T B W P N R L H B I
F S E H E U I E K E V
L A R H T N E Q V P I
Y F A C H E E R T O A
T S N S U O Y O J E L
D E T A R A L I H X E
T R R N L F H A P P Y
E A N O I T A L E L L
T E B U L L I E N T S
R V Q J J N S X S T C
O M D E I F I T A R G
F J R E T H G U A L C
M W T N E T N O C P F
O T H G I L E D L E X
C Q Y S A T S C E W Z
```

Were you right? Turn to page 182 for the answers

Wedding day

Do Catherine's butterflies mean she's making a big mistake?

The text message from Fiona said, "Why are you not at the house?" or, more precisely, "Y r u nt at da hse?"

Catherine sighed irritably as she deciphered the message. She was being summoned home by bad grammar. Not even bad grammar: it was nonsense. Even the word 'not' had been reduced to just two letters. Fiona had a degree in English – she, of all people, should have a respect for language! But after three years' studying, she was now willing to disregard spelling and grammar without a second thought.

"I'll be home in my own good time," Catherine responded. She inserted a full stop for good measure. "Put that in your pipe and smoke it," she thought smugly as she pressed the Send button.

The cool seawater gently washed over her rose-painted toenails. She liked the tickle of the sand between her toes. It was a bright morning and she could see for miles across the silver ocean. This was the morning of her wedding and the butterflies in her stomach felt more like cartwheeling monkeys. Sam, the little terrier that Tom had given her last year, scampered by her side.

Catherine was trembling. She thought of Tom. He was probably tucking into his daily breakfast of porridge at that moment. He was the sensible sort. He wouldn't let nerves interrupt his regular routine. Tom refused to do anything on an empty stomach.

She had escaped the house before anyone was up in an effort to calm her wedding-day jitters with a walk on the beach. She knew her jitters were unjustified because life without Tom was quite simply unthinkable.

Catherine's thoughts went back to their first meeting. When she had left school she had obtained a clerical job in London. At first, she detested her new life. She missed her parents and her friends, and longed for the familiar roar of the sea.

Then she met Tom. She was standing at the bus stop, snuggling down into the long scarf that her mother had knitted for her. He stood shivering next to her. "I could do with a scarf like that," he teased in a voice that was as warm as her favourite

coat. The morning city rush receded. There was something different about him. Something that to this day she could not explain. He had thick, wavy hair and misty green eyes. He laughed easily and made her laugh. They sat together on the 36 bus every morning through the month of February before he summoned up the courage to ask her for a date.

When he proposed, she had said yes without a second thought.

Last night, she and Fiona had drunk tea, nibbled digestive biscuits and discussed life. Catherine's simple silk dress with matching beaded bolero hung on the back of the door. "Are you excited?" Fiona cooed, her eyes wide with excitement. She was a hopeless romantic who longed to be swept away on a Hollywood cloud of passion. Catherine hoped that some day Fiona would find someone like Tom and discover what it was like to love with your soul as well as your heart.

The stroll along the beach had failed to settle Catherine's nerves. Her insides twisted at the thought of walking up the aisle with all eyes on her. She hated being the centre of attention and had always felt panicky when faced with life's major events. On her first day at school she had

> ## "There was something different about him... something that to this day she could not explain"

been sick all over the teacher's shoes.

With Sam at her heels, she made her way to the cave that had been her sanctuary since childhood and crept in. Sitting on one of the damp rocks, she closed her eyes and tried taking deep, calming breaths.

Suddenly, a warm familiar hand rested on her shoulder.

Tom smiled at her and said: "Fiona is going crazy. She says you disappeared from your room and haven't eaten any breakfast and the hairdresser is due at the house at any moment." He imitated Fiona's plaintive wail. Catherine

WORDS: JENNIFER KISSANE/ILLUSTRATION: KATE DAVIES

jitters

had to laugh and her nerves evaporated as he put his arm around her shoulder.

"How did you know I was here?" she asked.

He laughed: "Because this is where I found you 30 years ago when you also had a severe attack of nerves."

She giggled at the memory of a dishevelled Tom rushing in to her hideaway, already dressed in his morning suit. His young face had been wrinkled with worry and the fear of being abandoned on his wedding day. She looked at him now, thinking his eyes were as kind as ever and his love was like a suit of armour. Suddenly, Catherine

felt she could take on the whole world.

"You know," Tom mused, running his fingers through his greying hair, "you aren't supposed to be nervous about renewing your wedding vows, darling."

She shook her head defiantly. "I'm not nervous. Our daughter is being a drama queen."

Catherine held out her hand and Tom took it in his. He said softly: "Cathy, I could not imagine life without you – and I wouldn't want to."

She kissed his cheek lightly, her panic now turning to excitement, and replied: "Let's go and get married again!"

On the doorstep

Writer, Valery McConnell and **Yours** *readers remember when we welcomed the world on our doorstep*

I'm glad I can remember when milk was still delivered from a horse-drawn float, the bread man, coal man and paraffin man called regularly and Mum's groceries arrived weekly in a cardboard box from Mr Whiffin's. Those were the days when the commercial world was happy to come to your door. To me, one of the most interesting was the Betterware man. Dressed in a suit and hat, with a suitcase full of samples, he seldom left without an order from my mum – and she wasn't the only one.

"In the early Sixties, the Betterware man was a frequent visitor and I bought all my brushes from him," writes **Yvonne Parsons**.

"I still use the clothes brush on my husband's dinner jacket, the bath brush is still in use, as is my vegetable brush – all more than 50 years old." But perhaps even more surprising is how many of us remember our Betterware free gifts, from tiny tins of polish via plastic milk-bottle lids, to knitting needle gauges. When I recalled, from the Sixties, a free plastic coaster in the shape of a maple leaf, a large number of people sent me photos of the one that they still had – and, in one case, the coaster itself!

People talk of our modern consumer society, but back in the day it was amazing what you could buy on the doorstep. "I remember the tripe man coming to our door in Halifax," writes **Doreen Wardle**. "He had collapsible scales and weighed different types of tripe on a white pottery tray. Mum bought honeycomb tripe for Dad that he had with just salt and vinegar and another darker-looking type that she made into tripe and onions."

More tempting perhaps are **Barbara Weldrake's** memories of the crumpet man. "He would call with a wooden tray carried on his head with the crumpets covered by a white tea towel. We toasted them over the fire for a tea-time treat."

Marie Asher remembers the local hardware shop owner who, "would bring books of wallpaper samples to my door. You would order the paper and it would be delivered at no extra charge."

Harry Vinsome's farming uncle was, "too busy to go into town, so the tailor came to him. He chose the colour and material from a swatch, measurements were taken and the order completed with a handshake. Payment was only required when the customer was fully satisfied. Two weeks later the suit was delivered – a perfect fit!"

And you certainly met some characters this way. "The visitor I loved most of all was 'Auntie Annie', who would arrive every few weeks in a battered old Austin van," emails **Catherine Kidd**. "In exchange for old clothes and fabric my mother could choose pieces of second-

The bread man cometh… and the rest! We had lots of home deliveries growing up

The Betterware man came touting his wares… these days many of us have a sign to discourage doorstep salesmen

five old shillings – and a cuppa into the bargain."

"Quite regularly, men 'tramping' in the direction of London would knock on our front door and ask my mother if she would make them tea," writes **Olive Parry**. "The men gave Mom a 'mash' of tea leaves and sugar in a small bundle of paper. While Mom was making the tea the man often weeded the front garden, as a thank you. She always added a slice of cake, then gave him another bundle of tea and sugar and two pieces of thickly cut bread spread with dripping, to take on his way."

But in **Rita Holyoake's** household, it was their dog Brucie who gave the warmest welcome. "Brucie always waited at the side of the road for the butcher's van as the butcher always gave him a bone. One day it was raining hard and just as the butcher arrived, where Brucie sat patiently waiting, he heard a large clap of thunder. The lightning lifted Brucie into the air. Before the butcher could think about doing anything to help, Brucie had shook himself down and was standing on the bottom step of the van waiting for his meat bone as usual, none the worse for his adventure!"

As **Mrs G Smith** says, from the milkman to the rag-and-bone man, via the Breton onion seller... "These traders were the glue of society, dropping in for tea and a chat, keeping us well informed. How times have changed. I now have a door sign, provided by the police, to deter doorstep salesmen."

hand china and pots, all stacked in the van. My sister and I used to giggle uncontrollably as this rather large woman rummaged around in the van. She seemed oblivious to the fact that her large bloomers and stocking tops were very much on display!"

For many, including **Sue Dewhurst**, it was your first encounter with a member of the Sikh community. "An Indian man with a turban and huge moustache used to come once a year selling dusters, dishcloths and all sorts of colourful things.

Most of Mum's neighbours would just close the door in his face, but Mum always bought something and gave him juice and a slice of cake."

Glynis Allen's mum gave a warm welcome to Gypsy Rose Lee: "She would knock on the door three times (her magic number). She sold pegs and Nottingham lace and when she had your confidence she would say, 'I will read your palm for two bob or your tea leaves for half a crown'. My mother usually invited her in to read the tea leaves so she left with

A winter miracle

With no experience of dogs or children, can Imogen really help Ellie?

Drawing back the curtains in her sitting room, Imogen gazed with delight at the sight that met her eyes. It had snowed during the night and the frozen earth was covered with a crisp meringue of snow. Children were busily scooping up handfuls to build a snowman. Dogs skittered crazily in the unfamiliar white stuff. The sky was a cloudless blue and a solitary plane left a trail of silver vapour in its wake.

Imogen's eye was caught by the figure of little Ellie-Mae Parsons who lived in one of the old council houses on the other side of the village green. She was treading a solitary path accompanied only by a puppy, a long-legged creature of dubious parentage.

Ellie-Mae was a girl of whom Imogen was very fond. She was just such a child she would have liked as her own but, to her regret, marriage and babies had not come her way. Ellie was a plain little girl with dark eyes too large for her face and a shock of unruly hair, but with a sweet, loving nature that Imogen suspected was not appreciated at home.

As she watched, the child fell suddenly to her knees. She threw her arms around the dog and appeared to be crying. Opening the window and letting in a rush of icy air, Imogen called out: "Ellie - Ellie-Mae, come over here, dear."

Getting to her feet, the child made her way slowly, head hung down, towards the cottage. At the front door, she lifted a tear-stained face. "I can't come in, Miss Gray. I've got Buster and he's all wet. He'll make a mess in your house."

On cue, the puppy shook himself, sending particles of snow and ice in all directions. Ellie started to apologise but Imogen interrupted her with a laugh. "Don't worry, he's just making himself comfortable. Come along in, the pair of you."

She took Ellie's coat and put it to dry, then sat in a big armchair facing her. "Now, my dear, what are all these tears about?"

"It's Buster. Mum says I can't keep him now we've got a new baby. He's got to go and I shall never see him again." Her eyes filled with tears again as she spoke.

Imogen thought rapidly. She had as little experience of looking after dogs as children but she made a decision and asked impulsively: "Would you like me to look after him?"

Ellie's tear-filled eyes opened wide. "Oh, Miss Gray, would you? Would you really? He's ever so good - well, most of the time. I know he'd be good if he lived with you. Would you really have him?"

"Yes, I'd love to. As you know, I don't go out much these days but he can run round the garden and you could take him for walks so you'd see him every day. I'm sure that between us we could look after Buster and give him a happy life."

Ellie looked thoughtful for a moment, then said: "But he wouldn't really be my dog any more, would he? He'd be yours."

Imogen took Ellie's hand in hers. "Of course he'd still be your dog. I'd just be a sort of guardian."

The little girl still looked unsure, then said: "Perhaps he

Gray? You can have all my pocket money, but I don't think it would be enough. Buster does seem to eat a lot - Mum complained he sent her supermarket bills sky-high," she sighed. "I wish I was old enough to do a paper round or something."

"Now don't you worry yourself. You can be in charge of making sure he gets enough exercise and I'll be in charge of his food. After all, he is going to be our dog so I must do my part in his care."

Ellie's face lit up with a gap-toothed smile and, looking down at her, Imogen hoped that one day some discerning male would see the beauty of her character behind that rather plain little face and give her all the happiness she deserved.

Reaching up, Ellie put her arms round Imogen's neck and whispered: "Thank you, dear Miss Gray. I'm so glad Buster is coming to live with you and I can come here every day."

With the child's thin frame pressed lovingly to her, Imogen felt enveloped by a great glow of happiness. Soon, she was to have the company of a loveable puppy and daily visits from this equally loveable little girl.

Speaking softly, she asked: "Do you believe in miracles, Ellie?"

Ellie gave a deep sigh. "I do now, Miss."

"So do I, Ellie. So do I."

"What are all these tears about?"
"It's Buster - Mum says I can't keep him now we've got a new baby. He's got to go and I'll never see him again"

---

could be our dog, belonging to both of us?"

Imogen smiled: "That's a lovely idea. Would you like that, Buster?"

Buster thumped the floor enthusiastically with his stump of a tail. He behaved so nicely in her neat little cottage that Imogen forgot any qualms she might have had about taking on

a lively puppy.

After a mug of hot chocolate, Ellie went home with a happier heart. The next morning, she staggered over the green, loaded down with Buster's basket, toys and a large tin of dog food. Once again, her face wore a worried frown.

"What are we going to do about buying his food, Miss

Puzzle answers

PAGE 150

Crossword 1

ACROSS

1 Resume, 4 The Hague, 10 Toastmaster, 11 Née, 12 Easel, 13 Athletics, 14 Damsel, 16 Galleon, 18 Eve, 19 Damages, 21 Royale, 24 Chinatown, 26 Aloha, 27 Tie, 28 Muhammad Ali, 29 Resented, 30 Studio.

DOWN

1 Rotter, 2 Swansea, 3 Motel, 5 Hitch, 6 Horseplay, 7 Genuine, 8 Evensong, 9 Manacles, 15 Signalman, 16 Geronimo, 17 Educator, 20 Maidens, 22 Leopard, 23 Casino, 25 Ochre, 26 Adapt.

PAGE 158

Crossword 2

ACROSS

1 Walker, 4 Estimate, 9 Reward, 10 St Helens, 12 Rout, 13 Ferry, 14 Edge, 17 Ballpoint pen, 20 Mixed doubles, 23 Awry, 24 Salad, 25 Apse, 28 Rasputin, 29 Parrot, 30 Discount, 31 Campus.

DOWN

1 Wardrobe, 2 Lawfully, 3 Euro, 5 Saturated fat, 6 Idea, 7 Agenda, 8 Easter, 11 Deliberation, 15 Spain, 16 Seoul, 18 Claptrap, 19 Asbestos, 21 Hatred, 22 Crisis, 26 Sumo, 27 Papa.

PAGE 166

Crossword 3

ACROSS

1 Scrawl, 5 Single, 10 Hairbrush, 11 Toque, 12 Wellington boots, 13 Resign, 15 Severity, 17 Hail Mary, 19 Sphere, 23 The African Queen, 25 Ideal, 26 All Saints, 27 Osprey, 28 Detail.

DOWN

2 Chill, 3 Ambling, 4 Lounge, 5 Schooner, 6 Notable, 7 Liquorice, 8 Shower, 9 Measly, 14 Spineless, 16 Ordinary, 17 Hot air, 18 Muffler, 20 Piquant, 21 Ernest, 22 Ballad, 24 Ennui.

PAGE 174

Crossword 4

ACROSS

3 Eurythmics, 8 Reflex, 9 Galactic, 10 Tommyrot, 11 Crisis, 12 Majestic, 15 Barmaid, 17 Scandal, 19 Noisiest, 21 Sticky, 25 North Sea, 26 Hat trick, 27 Walker, 28 On the cards.

DOWN

1 Detour, 2 Climbs, 3 Expressive, 4 Ragtime, 5 Till, 6 Moccasin, 7 Chilli, 11 Cabin, 13 Jackstraws, 14 Coley, 16 Mismatch, 18 Stinker, 20 Obtain, 22 Inhale, 23 Keeper, 24 Disc.

Wordsearch 1

Wordsearch 2

Wordsearch 3

Wordsearch 4